THE
ELEVATOR
SPEECH

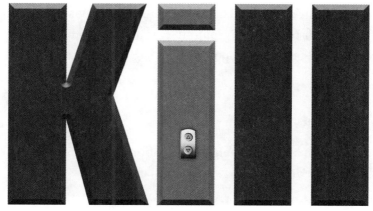

THE
ELEVATOR
SPEECH

Stop Selling, Start Connecting

FELICIA J. SLATTERY M.A., M.Ad.Ed.

Sound Wisdom

P.O. Box 310

Shippensburg, PA 17257-0310

For more information on foreign distribution, call 717-530-2122.
Reach us on the Internet: www.soundwisdom.com.

ISBN 13 TP: 978-0-7684-0784-6

ISBN 13 HC: 978-1-937879-10-5

ISBN 13 Ebook: 978-1-937879-11-2

For Worldwide Distribution, Printed in the U.S.A.

1 2 3 4 5 6 7 8 / 18 17 16 15

DEDICATION

I dedicate this book to my mother-in-law and father-in-law, Anne and Richard Parkhill, who never met a stranger. I wish I could show the world your warmth and kindness whenever you meet others. You are the model of what living life without needing an elevator speech is all about: connecting with people in meaningful ways. Thank you for the gift of your son and your presence in my life. I love you.

I also dedicate this book to business professionals around the world who have always felt like that darn elevator speech thing wasn't right for you. You were right. I hope the ideas in this book free you to connect authentically from your real self and enjoy networking forever and always. Meeting new friends is fun and I hope to meet you soon, too!

CONTENTS

Signature Speech is my trademarked name for the system I will explain in Part Three of this book. Any use of the term is strictly enforced as I consider it the cornerstone of my business communication philosophy.

FOREWORD

The very idea of networking often makes people cringe. Why wouldn't you, if you look at networking as the old-school business mentality of meet-and-greet events where everyone's goal is to schmooze and manipulate each other to see who can crush the competition? Ugh. No wonder people hate the idea. It's uncomfortable and self-serving and downright deceptive at times.

The new reality of networking is that it's all about making lasting connections, regardless if any of those connections themselves ever buy anything from you. It means bringing value to each other.

When you're building your business, if you're very clear on who you want to work with, who is your ideal client, your business will thrive. The right clients are the clients who will energize and inspire you. The clients who make work seem like fun. If you're looking to meet more people like that, you need something far beyond an elevator speech because of course not everyone you meet will be a good fit, but they can be someone who you give value to, who will remember you, and who just might be able to introduce you to someone else in their network who would be your most amazing, ideal client.

I've asked audiences for years how many love, love, love listening to someone else's elevator speech and how many love giving their own elevator speech. No one's hands ever go up. People still teach it because of course we need to be able to talk about our businesses. This book, *Kill the Elevator Speech: Stop Selling, Start Connecting,* opens the door to meeting people and talking about your business in an entirely new and fun way that feels real, allows others to be themselves, and helps you to relax and enjoy meeting people. As you exchange your stories, that opens the door to continuing the relationship and expanding both your networks. In the 21st century, we work in a world where relationships matter above all else.

In *Kill the Elevator Speech: Stop Selling, Start Connecting,* Felicia Slattery provides you with a simple and unique five-word question to help you break the ice with anyone, anywhere, at any time. This book boils the five-part "Book Yourself Solid Dialog" I've written about into its essence: to have a real conversation and connect with someone as a human being instead of as a walking, talking, arrogant "all-about-me" jerk. You'll discover how to actually listen to the other person you're meeting and how to respond to the person in a way that can become the building blocks of a professional relationship.

Beyond networking and the elevator speech, even, there is so much more you can do to bring in more clients. In fact, I've long been a proponent of doing what Felicia calls "serving your audience from the stage." With my background in acting, I now host small retreats and larger workshops to show experts and speakers how to rise above the crowd of other speakers and provide a real experience for their audiences so those audiences sit up and take notice. I believe the honor of performing for, speaking to, or teaching an audience full of people is about the biggest gift you'll ever be given. In the section that covers Felicia's trademarked "Signature Speech" system, she presents precisely how you can use the power of public speaking to engage your audiences both in person and virtually using the tools available to you for free on the Internet.

It's time we all kill the elevator speech. This book will help you. Let's get out there and build value for others while truly connecting with them.

Think big.

MICHAEL PORT
New York Times best-selling author of five books,
including *Book Yourself Solid* and *The Think Big Manifesto*

Introduction

Kill the Elevator Speech

The book you now hold in your hands has been in progress for quite some time. Why? Because I was forced to take an indefinite break from writing it. Well, actually, life pretty much forced me to take a break from everything for a while. But more on that later.

First, a little background on how this book came to be in the first place.

"You Took the Words Right Out of My Mouth!"

The idea for this book came from an event in October 2011, where *New York Times* best-selling author of *Book Yourself Solid*, Michael Port, and I were both speaking. During his presentation, Michael told the audience that he was on a mission to "kill the elevator speech." I was sitting in the back row of the theater-style auditorium near the other speakers. Now, imagine if you will, the sound of a record screeching to a stop mid-song, because that's exactly what I heard in my mind when Michael made that statement, followed quickly by the sound of angels singing a hallelujah chorus. I was struck like lightning, and just as electrified!

Finally! I had my answer!

As a professional communication strategist and speech coach for clients in countries all around the world, for years clients and colleagues had asked me about helping them write this horrendous "elevator speech." But all the while, I had firmly believed that this prehistoric type of "communication"—if you can even call it that—should never be used by any human being who wants to truly connect with another person. People urged me to teach a course or offer a consulting session to help them write their elevator speeches. But in good conscience I just could not. You'll read all the reasons why as you delve into this book.

Now, finally, here was Michael Port, a well-respected, mega-successful author and consultant, speaking my truth for all to hear. Outside of social media, I had never met him before that event, but I knew at that moment I'd be grateful to him forever!

THE RIGHT BOOK AT THE RIGHT TIME

This book was definitely meant to be. About a month or so after that lightning bolt moment in the auditorium, my now publisher, Nathan Martin of Sound Wisdom Publishing (who at the time I had also never met), reached out to me to review another of their author's books.

I took the opportunity to set up a meeting to share with him the idea for my own book idea, *Kill the Elevator Speech*. They accepted my book idea almost immediately! That was early December 2011. As I worked on the book over the next few months, I was suddenly hit with a late winter cold and cough. That cough soon turned into such a severe case of pneumonia that I had to be hospitalized for five full days—a day longer than the typical pneumonia.

Although I was released from the hospital, my chest x-rays curiously never cleared up. Specialists assured me that, because the pneumonia was so severe, there was bound to be a lot of "junk" my lungs had to clear out and that could take some time. So they kept following up with continued x-rays every few weeks. When there was still no improvement two months out of the hospital, they decided a CT scan was in order.

That CT scan showed the same thing: a big hunk of "something not right" where my right lung should be. Because I had no risk factors for any type of lung disease beyond a mild case of asthma, and due to my age (I was only 42 at the time), they still believed it was the severe pneumonia clearing up. More follow-up tests, with more x-rays ordered, were scheduled in another six weeks.

By the end of the summer, I was feeling well, outside of minor discomfort when breathing deeply (that definitely felt wrong). When another x-ray showed still no further improvement, doctors decided to take more definitive and surgical steps to figure out the mystery.

During two bronchoscopies—a surgical "look-see" down my windpipe into the entrance to my lung—a tumor was discovered. The first biopsy came back that the tissue was benign, but later tests confirmed the worst. With zero risk factors, i.e., I had never smoked a day in my life or lived or worked with smokers, never lived or worked near asbestos, and had no radon exposure, at age 42, on September 20, 2012, I was diagnosed with lung cancer.

You'd think that diagnosis would feel like a punch to the gut, but for me it was a relief. After months of not knowing what was wrong with me, finally I had answers—even if they weren't exactly great ones!

And medical science had a well-laid-out path for me that included surgery, which removed the middle lobe and small section of the lower lobe of my right lung, and completely cured the cancer without any need for the horrible radiation or chemotherapy so many people need when diagnosed with cancer.

LIFE—AND CAREER—INTERRUPTED

Recovery was long and painful, and for a while, I wondered if I would need to find a new line of work. I could barely speak a sentence without coughing or hacking. There was simply no way I could get on a stage or even run a webinar. However, after three months of physical therapy and lots of prayers from around the world, my voice and energy returned better than ever.

You'd think that would be the end of the story, but it wasn't. After a few months of roaring back to work and overdoing it on staying healthy, I was struck again, this time with kidney stones, and was out of work for two more months dealing with painful infections, and more surgeries for treatment. Apparently that green smoothie craze should be done in moderation. Oh well, live and learn.

And so now, I've been back to work, writing and speaking again. The time is now for killing the elevator speech. I've come back from kicking cancer to the curb to make sure we kick elevator speeches to the curb. I'm on a mission and I won't stop until elevator speeches are like dinosaurs: something for the history books but nothing that people have to experience today. Thank you for joining me on this mission to *Kill the Elevator Speech,* once and for all:

LET'S KILL THE ELEVATOR SPEECH!

I realize that "killing the elevator speech" may sound a bit extreme and controversial. But wait, before you get your business undies in a bunch, especially if you're an "old school" business person who learned about running a business long before the days of the Internet and social media, relax. It's really for the best and *not* quite as extreme as it sounds.

You might be tempted to get huffy with me and immediately dismiss, or even dislike, this book. And if you're someone who's *taught* others how to write and deliver a "killer" elevator speech, no shame can come to you because we've *all* been taught we must have an elevator speech in order to succeed. How else would we tell people who we are and what we do when we meet them?

For decades, an elevator speech has been considered a crucial "quick communication" tool, like a business card. If you don't have the basic tools, or so goes the typical wisdom, including an elevator speech, you might as well not bother going to a networking meeting, and maybe even think twice about this whole business professional thing being for you.

FIRST, LET'S UNDERSTAND THE ELEVATOR SPEECH

Before going on, here is a common definition of an elevator speech as it appears on Wikipedia.com, "An *elevator pitch* is a summary used to quickly and simply define a product, service, or organization and its value proposition. The name 'elevator pitch' reflects the idea that it should be possible to deliver the summary in the time span of an elevator ride, or approximately thirty seconds to two minutes."

What's the first thing you notice about that definition? Well, that it's not intended to be a "speech" at all. It's also known as a "pitch." And the idea is that the person you're delivering it to will be in a position to buy your product or service—and that, by necessity, your elevator speech will give that person enough information to make a decision about wanting to know more.

Yes, there are more detailed descriptions available, and we will delve into some of those in the rest of this book. I chose this description because it best exemplifies the way that most people with planned elevator speeches network to find business or a job.

BUSINESS AS USUAL OR BETTER BUSINESS?

If you're worried about not having what you've always known to be an essential business tool, take a deep breath and allow for the *possibility* that something *even better* exists. After all, there are no "speech police" and you don't have to do everything I'll share with you in this book. It's still a free country and you're "free" to stay on the beaten path.

If you read this book and still prefer to deliver your tired, old elevator speech then, sadly, I will have failed in my mission. But I think that, if you're willing to entertain the idea of "what if" that I present in the following pages, you'll see a better alternative for doing business in the modern world.

Remember, it's a risk-free enterprise: you read the book and decide for yourself if the path I offer is right or wrong for you. After the last page, you're free to conduct business as usual—or better business.

Again, your choice.

However, you may also fall into another camp. You might be the business professional who either had training on writing and delivering your elevator speech, but haven't quite been able to pull it off, or have felt guilty because you haven't even bothered to try.

After all, "everybody" knows you *have* to have an elevator speech, right? Yet something about it may not have felt quite right. Not quite like "you." Maybe not even "real." If that is the case, then this book is for you, so you can finally breathe a sigh of relief.

Your instincts were right after all. You *don't* need an elevator speech, particularly if it always felt clunky, salesy, and even a little bit smarmy rolling—or stumbling—off your tongue. There is something far better that will allow you to feel more like the real you when you meet people, which will allow you to express yourself—your true self—in a way that leads to active, effective communication.

The kind that gets results and keeps getting results.

FIVE LITTLE WORDS: THE SECRET TO KILLING YOUR ELEVATOR SPEECH

As I explained in the previous section, this book was inspired by a speech given by *New York Times* best-selling author Michael Port, in which he talked about some of the content in his book. If you've not yet read Michael Port's *Book Yourself Solid*,[1] add that to your reading list immediately and fast-track it to the top!

In *Book Yourself Solid* you'll see that Port agrees with me that, if we're in any kind of business, *of course* we have to be able to talk about our professions and businesses. We simply have to have a way to share what we do. While Port provides one conversational alternative in his book, this book addresses the question, "What could one do instead of delivering an elevator speech?"

What's more, it proposes *five simple words* to remember to ask others the next time you're at a networking meeting, conference, seminar, school reunion, family function, or anywhere you meet people and might otherwise be tempted to ask, "What do you do?"

In Part One of this book, we'll examine the origin and history of the elevator speech and why many well-meaning "experts" are still teaching the elevator speech even though the ways of doing business have changed. Finally you'll see why, based on empirical research in various fields, the elevator speech is outdated and does not work to establish the desired beginnings of a relationship. Part One ends with a real solution for how to get the conversation and the human connection working in that moment of meeting another person.

In Part Two, we will look at which solutions will help you to establish and build professional relationships without the elevator speech. Part Two will also shows you how to easily and efficiently go above and beyond simple tricks and tactics so you can truly connect with your fellow human beings in a meaningful way. Social media, public speaking, and discovering how to ask better questions are all presented for you so you can easily connect with anyone, in any walk of life, at any time.

Throughout the pages of this book, you'll meet some interesting characters, including some best-selling authors and successful business people who all understand the elevator speech should be a thing of the past.

You'll also meet historical figures, including one of the founders of the United States of America, Benjamin Franklin, in a surprising role. I refer to Franklin as the "Grandfather of Networking and Masterminding" (and you thought it was Napoleon Hill!).

Also from history, you'll meet Alexis de Tocqueville, the French aristocrat who came to the US in the 1830s to learn about American social and political institutions, calling America "a nation of joiners." You'll discover how the lessons of nearly two centuries ago still apply to the way we do business today.

PARTING WORDS

The foundations of this book come from more than 25 years of studying human communication, teaching communication and speaking skills, consulting with clients around the world, and sharing from stages coast to coast, virtually and via broadcast media. The goal is to help others kill the elevator speech so we all can stop "selling" and start truly connecting and establishing fulfilling relationships that lead to greater sales and wealth of all kinds.

If you want better business relationships, you've found the right book.

If you want more confidence, clarity, and brevity when stating your case—when stating any case—you're in the right place.

And if you're ready to get started, all you need to do is turn the page...

ENDNOTE

1. Michael Port, *Book Yourself Solid* (Hoboken, NJ: Wiley, 2010).

PART ONE

ORIGINS OF THE ELEVATOR SPEECH

CHAPTER 1

ELEVATOR SPEECH HISTORY

"A business professional walks into a bar…"

No, this is not the beginning of a bad joke. Although, it could feel like it on any given "after hours" evening at a networking function. Instead, it's merely the beginning of what most of us simply call "networking."

In today's modern, fast-paced world, business professionals meet at networking events anywhere and anytime: before, during, and after work hours, at night and on the weekends, at restaurants, hotel conference rooms, convention centers, on golf courses, local and out-of-town meetings, local business shops, chambers of commerce offices, and yes, even at bars. They also meet at family functions like weddings, barbecues, picnics, dinner parties, and on vacations.

People meet everywhere, all the time; it's just part of what we do. It's "why" we do it that I'd like to discuss in this first chapter.

WHY NETWORKING?

I once had a reporter ask me why it's so important to always be networking. I don't recall exactly what I said at the time, but it comes down to the fact that, boiled down to its most basic element, "networking" is simply *meeting people and getting to know more about them.* Simple, right? I wish!

But let's back up: Why network in the first place? Why go to all this trouble of handshaking and storytelling and elevator pitching? The fact is, as human beings, we can't *not* network. It's part of our nature, our collective DNA, as social beings. From caves to campfires to tribes to villages to towns to cities to social media, we are and have always been social creatures, personally and professionally.

It's a fact that businesses of all kinds, no matter the size, from shoestring start-ups to major conglomerates, are started, run, staffed, and supported by people. All sorts of people. And guess who keep these businesses, big and small, in business? That's right—more people.

Meeting other people and learning about their various skill sets, talents, products, services, needs, and goals is how we build, grow, or change our business in a positive way. We may end up hiring those people, selling something to those people, buying from those people, referring business to or having business referred from those people.

But the glue that binds us all together is our humanity. We are all people, plain and simple. Each of us has our own dreams and goals, desires and needs, plans and problems, successes and failures, heroes and villains, insecurities and confidences, faith and freedoms, and preferences and dislikes. They are what make us unique as individuals, and what ties us together as a race.

To every interaction, conversation, or introduction, we bring with us our emotions, knowledge, backgrounds, education, professional experience, political beliefs, religious or spiritual beliefs and practices, family situations, health needs, and past and current challenges. Some call this emotional "baggage," but that tends to have a negative connotation, so I just call it...luggage.

We each bring our emotional "luggage" to every encounter we have with other people, who also bring their "luggage" to the encounter making every human interaction the emotional equivalent of one of those rotating conveyor belts at the luggage claim at the airport! And then we're expected to communicate. Ha! It's a wonder any of us ever get our meanings across, let alone walk away from an interaction without completely offending the other person.

Throughout our history, human communication has remained essentially the same. We each bring our "luggage" to every encounter, and we then have to get down to the business of understanding the other person and being understood ourselves. In looking back through time, we can see that although it seems everything in business has changed, the essence of how real work gets done has stayed the same.

PLANES, TRAINS, AND...LIGHT BULBS

No one knows who delivered the first elevator pitch, but its origins are said to have emerged from the high-risk, high-stakes world of angel investors and venture capitalists. Typically angel investors, who get their name from a term that began during the golden age of Broadway musicals beginning in the 1920s, are wealthy individuals who invest their own money in start-up businesses because of their interest in and personal affinity for the business idea, the entrepreneur, or both. Venture capitalists, on the other hand, are larger organizations that provide capital funding for companies to support infrastructure, factory building, staffing and the like and involve greater control in the overall operations of the companies in which they invest. Both require potential "investees" to pitch them information about the investment potential.

In the early half of the 20th century, as the industrial revolution was firmly underway in the United States, wealthy families increased their wealth by funding start-up companies and new ideas they were excited about and/or found worthwhile. You may recognize the names Vanderbilt, Rockefeller, Whitney, and Morgan as families whose money, ideas, and entrepreneurial spirit helped build America from frontier land into capitalist superpower.

The next time you drive your car across town or step into an airplane, you can thank the Rockefellers for investing in oil refineries and the airline industry; the next time you turn on your lights or plug in your laptop, you can thank J.P. Morgan for investing in Thomas Edison's inventions; and when you hop on a train, give a nod, or possibly a shout-out, to the Vanderbilts.

Planes, trains, automobiles, and light bulbs, among thousands of other inventions and innovations we use today, came as a direct result of the investment of some of these American business pioneers and the funds they contributed to would-be inventors, entrepreneurs, and thought leaders.[1]

How people would get their money from those wealthy men varied. For example, Thomas Edison did receive money from J.P. Morgan after giving an impassioned speech. But it was no elevator pitch; it was more of a press conference.[2]

On September 15, 1878, Edison invited a group of reporters to visit his laboratory in Menlo Park, New Jersey, where he made a bold announcement. He told the reporters gathered that in just six weeks he would make the gaslight industry obsolete because he was going to create another industry to provide electric power that would revolutionize America and light up the world.

He proclaimed, "When I am through, only the rich will be able to afford candles." Overnight, gas stocks plummeted and John Pierpont Morgan, better known as J.P. Morgan, the millionaire banker, financier, art collector, and philanthropist, rushed to meet with Edison and invest in his project. In 1881, Morgan was rewarded by having his 219 Madison Avenue house, the first private residence in New York City, fully illuminated by electric lights.[3]

That important part of history (when the Edison Electric Light Company was financed by Morgan and those he advised to invest money, including the Vanderbilt family) came about from a speech and from personal human connection. Yet Edison did not give an elevator speech of any kind, but an actual speech to the news media, which got the attention of the wealthy investor, leading to a meeting, where neither had to introduce himself to the other, and the investment being made.[4]

MORE FUNDS, MORE BUSINESS GROWTH

One of the first investors to give money to start-up businesses became known as the "father of venture capitalism," Georges Doriot. Doriot was born in France in 1899, later emigrated to the United States in 1921 to study business at Harvard University and became a military general during World War II.

"The General," as he was called during the war due to his rank and later as a sign of respect, began teaching at Harvard. In 1946, while dean of the Harvard University School of Business, he was simultaneously hired to lead the first publicly owned venture capital firm, American Research and Development Corporation (ARDC).

This is notable because suddenly, for the first time, entrepreneurs could turn to a source outside of wealthy individuals to invest in their ideas. To be funded by the ARDC, Doriot believed *a person's character was just as important*, if not more so than his business acumen, saying, "a creative man merely has ideas; a resourceful man makes them practical."[5]

To be funded by ARDC, an entrepreneur or group had to send a project write-up to the venture capitalist firm. It was the writing, not the speaking, that got them in the door. But it was *who they were as a person* that finally won the successful candidates the funding they needed for their projects.

Surprisingly, despite how many years have passed, not much has changed in the world of networking today: it's who you are as a person—that "luggage" or emotional "everything" you bring into every interaction—that will ultimately get you to success in any aspect of what you do.

THE PATH TO BUSINESS FINANCING: FIVE WAYS TO FUND YOUR PROFESSIONAL DREAMS

When folks with a big idea need funding to get their businesses off the ground, they have a few notable options (some of which you may have even tried before):

1. Finance the project on their own through their personal savings and other accumulated wealth.

2. Borrow money from family/friends (an idea that is always fraught with potential holiday-table conversation danger!).

3. Use credit cards and have to pay them off for the next 37 years with interest totaling an amount likely millions of dollars more than what was charged to begin with.

4. Get a loan from a bank—and jump through 8,239 hoops to get it, usually with insane interest rates, if you're even approved at all.

5. Find private investors, called venture capitalists (or "VCs," for short) or angel investors, to fully fund your business, so you can turn a profit, repay your investors and then some (i.e., put a roof over your head, eat, and possibly go out to a movie once in a while!).

In any of these scenarios, other than using your own financing or credit cards (Egads!), to get your foot in the door, you would have to be able to succinctly share your business idea and why it might be a good, low-risk investment.

THE EVOLUTION OF THE ELEVATOR SPEECH

So, the "elevator speech" came about because VCs, being successful in business and busy people themselves, have little time to listen to long pitches from hopeful entrepreneurs, who would love nothing more than to spend an entire afternoon explaining why their pet rock is better than that "other" pet rock!

The VCs decide quickly whether or not they want to even see a proposal or have a meeting. They will also decide—just as quickly—if the idea is not one that will work for them for any number of reasons, many of which having nothing to do with the pitch itself. For instance, maybe the idea is for a widget, but this VC only funds services; maybe the idea is for a retail outlet, but that VC only funds restaurants; maybe the scope of the business idea is national, but that VC only funds local or international businesses, etc.

The elevator speech was born out of the concept that as a business person with a great new idea going in front of very busy people with lots of money but limited time, you have about the time it would take to pitch your idea had you been lucky enough to *end up in an elevator* with an actual venture capitalist. (How would you spot one? Who knows, maybe they wear special hats or green armbands with dollar signs on them so the rest of us mere mortals can easily spot them?)

Real or imagined, if you were to have captured the attention of a VC—hopefully not trapped in an elevator like a lion in a cage—you would still need to make your "pitch" between the time when the imaginary elevator doors closed and when the VC would get off the elevator a few floors up.

That means, according to most sources, you would have about 30 seconds to perhaps two minutes (depending on if there was a monkey pulling the make-believe lift or not and on how high you were going in the building) to tell the story of your business idea and why you were deserving of the person's money. During those precious seconds, you had to dazzle, impress, and just plain WOW that VC into not only wanting to know more, but ultimately writing you a check for your most excellent business idea.

As business moved forward, the concept of the elevator speech has come to mean something very specific:

> The words used to introduce oneself and one's professional agenda that should take about 30 seconds to two minutes, which is the time it would take from getting on to an elevator to getting off that elevator at another floor. The speech, a marketing tool, should be compelling enough to lead to more conversation and possibly doing business together.

In fact, there are many who argue that regardless of your occupation, even if you have a job and are happily working, if you happen to get onto the elevator in your office building with the CEO or upper-level management, you should have an "elevator speech" prepared that explains what project you're working on, what progress you're making on that project, and how that project will benefit the company.

Now, doesn't *that* sound like fun?

REALITY CHECK: FACT VERSUS FICTION

Let's pause in our dramatic and sweeping history of the elevator speech for a brief reality check. Just a quick show of hands, how many times have you gotten into an elevator with a stranger and had *any* kind of conversation whatsoever, beyond perhaps some basic banter about which floor they were going to and after an awkward silence, the weather?

Or:

How many times have you been in the presence of a VC, either inside or outside an elevator, who would be ready to write you a big, fat, juicy check after a 30-second pitch?

Or:

How many times have you been in the situation where the leader of your organization stepped onto an elevator with you and asked you how XYZ project is going? And how many times, if that might ever happen, would you really not know how to answer without a planned speech?

None? Oh, really? Huh, go figure.

Then…what is the elevator speech for? Who is it for? And why are we still using…

But wait, I'm getting ahead of myself. The truth of the matter is you're not getting onto random elevators, not even hotel elevators when you're at a conference or convention or the elevators at the office building, and trying to sell anyone anything. The idea of meeting someone and then 30 seconds later having them whip out their wallets to give you cash is preposterous in any legal business setting and might only happen in the movies.

Yes, I'm passionate about this topic. Yes, I can get fired up. Yes, it's my own personal and professional soapbox. And yes, I may be a bit cynical about all this…but you would be too if you recognized that we are all being continually accosted by this speech that is *so wrong!*

It is true that if you are in the market for a VC to fund your project, you will need something juicy get their attention. Yet none of the VCs I interviewed or researched for this book want to be introduced to you verbally first. Most prefer an email with specific information about the project as a way to filter out ideas that may not work for them. So the elevator pitch, even in its original context, becomes a moot point, particularly in this day and age of email, text, and social media.

However, most people in business are not in that situation, and in fact will never meet a VC in their lives, and therefore do not need any kind of pitch for that scenario.

So, again, why the elevator speech?!

SHOCKING TRUTHS REVEALED: THE REAL PURPOSE OF THE ELEVATOR SPEECH

But wait, if you've been tricked into believing that you "MUST" have an elevator speech in order to succeed in business, you're potentially arguing right now that the purpose of the elevator speech isn't to make people whip out their wallets, but only to get a conversation started. And if so, thank you, because you're actually making my point. Here's how: Most of the newer books and articles on updating the old-fashioned elevator speech "the right way" and bringing it into the 21st century business world are not about having someone buy from you right away, but about being intriguing, standing out, having a personal brand, being polarizing to make a strong—and lasting—first impression.

The new elevator speech teachers want you to be pithy, witty, persuasive, and creative enough to inspire the poor soul on the receiving end to ask you for more information and to set up a meeting with you. That's a tall order. That's also just plain wrong on multiple levels. If the purpose of your first bits of dialog with another human being is opening and continuing a friendly, two-way dialogue, then giving a concise speech from a "thought-provoking" bit of prose written to pique a person's curiosity isn't going to cut it.

The reason why boils down to interpersonal communication.

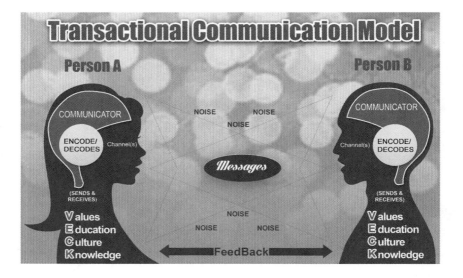

How Communication Works

In the transactional model of communication, as you can see in Figure 1, there is a person with an idea, called Person A in the model. That person has to get his or her idea across to another person, Person B. Both people have their own unique individual backgrounds represented in Figure 1 as VECK on both sides: Values, Education, Culture, and Knowledge, which equal the sum of his or her experience and environment.

The message, in this case a personal introduction, has to get from Person A to Person B through some way, called a channel. In a face-to-face networking situation, that channel is talking. Yet there are other challenges all around called "noise" that make it difficult to fully listen and engage with the other person's message.

There is more in a later chapter on listening and noise, but for now, know that there is both *internal noise*—our thoughts, feelings, preoccupations, etc.—and *external noise,* such as other people talking or an airplane flying overhead.

This noise can also interfere with both the sending and receiving of the message. The last part of the model includes continuous feedback, both in verbal and nonverbal ways.

PARTING WORDS

In later chapters we'll look at what you can do and say to communicate that you are a real, true, and—dare I use the hot buzz term of our current era—"authentic" person there to meet others in the hopes that you might have a mutually beneficial relationship. People will see that you're not there to "work the numbers," but to meet people. I'll tell you this: it ain't the "elevator speech."

Because the elevator speech has problems, big ones. Six of them, to be exact.

ENDNOTES

1. http://www.pbs.org/wnet/historyofus/web10/features/bio/B14
    .html; accessed June 7, 2014. Charles R. Morris, *The Tycoons: How Andrew Carnegie, John D. Rockefeller, Jay Gould, and J. P. Morgan Invented the American Supereconomy* (New York: MacMillan, 2010).

2. http://www.pbs.org/wgbh/amex/edison/filmmore/description
    .html; accessed June 7, 2014.

3. Herbert I. Satterlee, *J. Pierpont Morgan: An Intimate Portrait* (New York: MacMillan Company, 1939), 190, 207, 212.

4. "Edison's Miracle of Light," PBS Television Series: *The American Experience.*

5. Andrew Beattie, "Georges Doriot and the Birth of Venture Capital," January 26, 2010; Investopedia; http://www .investopedia.com/articles/financialcareers/10/georges-doriot -venture-capital.asp; accessed August 20, 2013. S.E. Ante, Creative Capital: *Georges Doriot and the Birth of Venture Capital* (Boston: Harvard Business School Press, 2008).

CHAPTER 2

How to Solve Six Elevator Speech Problems

In the fall of 2012, after I had major, open-lung surgery, part of my three-month recovery included a significant amount of physical therapy. The location I chose was close to my home, which made going there three to four times per week for hours at a time very convenient. Based on the couple of times I had taken loved ones to physical therapy appointments in the past, the atmosphere of this particular location was unlike how I'd imagined it would be.

Rather than some sterile, nursing home-type environment, it was set up like a small gym or personal training studio that included an area with about eight tables for the therapists to work on individual patients. Because so many of us were there for two or more hours at a time—some were there for five hours at a stretch!—I started to see many of the same faces over and over again.

I quickly noticed that part of the culture of that physical therapy location was for the multiple therapists on duty at the time, along with the "regular" patients, including myself, to banter back and forth, talk about sports (a big thing when you live in the Chicago area and one of the guys in therapy alongside you is a professional athlete), and laugh at ourselves and our circumstances.

I began to think of it as "laughing through the pain."

Of course, part of the conversation and small talk revolved around meeting each other, shaking hands, and introducing ourselves. In such an intimate setting, it just felt "right" to get to know each other better. As part of that process, inevitably someone would ask, "So what do you do for a living?"

If I wasn't already against using an elevator speech, I might have had a problem given my "target" audience at the time. Many of the folks in physical therapy with me at that time were heavy laborers of some kind: truck drivers, brick layers, etc.

There was also a nurse, a professional athlete, a grocery store check-out person—all of whom had been injured while on the job. Then there were a couple of people like me who weren't injured on the job, but had surgery or some other injury from which they were recovering.

Just imagine the look on the face of a big, 50-something Teamsters truck driver walking the treadmill recovering from a knee injury after he asked me, "What do you do?" and I gave him a pat "elevator speech" answer. I would have been laughed right out of the place (and rightfully so)! Or worse, he would have been confused or weirded out and probably just walked away, never to speak to me again. I would quickly become a pariah in the physical therapy studio.

Now, I know what you may be thinking, that you have to be "strategic" when deciding if you're going to use your elevator speech or not. That it's not a one-size-fits-all, template kind of scenario. Obviously, the physical therapy studio wasn't the place, the time, or the audience for any kind of pre-programmed "pitch."

It certainly wasn't a networking type of meeting place. No one goes to physical therapy with the express purpose of meeting other professional people with whom to do business or refer to others. But that's one of the several problems with why the elevator speech stinks on so many levels. This chapter covers many others. Why should we have to "be strategic" in our relationships? Why can't we simply "meet" people without expecting anything from them? That seems like a lot of undue stress and extra decision-making steps that don't need to exist.

TELLING YOUR STORY

Pulitzer Prize winner Tracy Kidder, co-author of *Good Prose: The Art of Nonfiction*,[1] says, "I tend to worry now when a story is easily summarized and in summary sounds interesting, or, even worse, exciting."

Put into the context of introducing yourself, which in itself is telling your own story, if you can boil down all that you do—all that you are—into an exciting few words, that almost trivializes what you do, your background, history, experience, and who you are. It's one thing to tell a friend about a book or movie with a simple, "It's like Avatar meets Star Wars" tag line, but it's quite another when you're trying to do the same for yourself!

When you take the complex systems you use in every aspect of your professional life, from booking appointments, to making phone calls, sending and checking email, connecting with people on social media, serving clients, selling products and services, creating products and services, and so much more—to sum all of that up into a few pithy phrases designed to get a reaction from another person takes the full value of what you bring to the table and completely undermines it.

Why? Why do we bother? Because we always have? Because some professor in the first class of our business degree told us we should? When a complex idea or set of actions or solution to a problem can be boiled down quickly and made to sound exciting, you could be using great marketing and speech techniques, but you've also likely lost the essence, nuances, and true uniqueness of the experience you're trying to represent with just a few words.

In later chapters we'll deal with telling your story in a way that makes sense and invites others to do the same, creating the basis for a much more fulfilling conversation. But for now, I want to focus on how *not* to tell your story, on how *not* to summarize, boil down, encapsulate, or "tag line" yourself into a corner. In other words, I want to talk about what's wrong with the elevator speech.

There are dozens of books in which well-meaning authors teach you how to use an elevator speech. Not surprisingly, the authors of those same books get on national TV, are interviewed for business magazines, and hired to speak on stages from coast to coast and around the English-speaking world.

But it is my firm opinion that those smart folks are making a huge mistake in leading business professionals down the path of thinking that having one singular statement to introduce themselves is going to get them ahead.

When, unfortunately, it won't. It just won't.

WHO SUPPOSEDLY "NEEDS" AN ELEVATOR SPEECH ANYWAY?

Like a business card, a well-written resume, and a good suit, professionals are told almost from day one of business school and work that they also need an elevator speech as a tool to be successful in business. Well-meaning "experts" in all types of industries—from marketing to education to entrepreneurs and beyond—have bastardized the idea of having a 30-second to two-minute "pitch" for a venture capitalist into using the elevator speech in all different kinds of contexts.

A quick Internet search reveals not only business professionals, but people from all walks of life being instructed on how to deliver a speech at cocktail parties and at business conferences alike, to include:

- Graduate students currently in school

- Employees of companies (occasionally referred to as "intrapreneurs")

- Entrepreneurs and small business owners

- Salespeople

- Consultants

- Inventors

- Product producers

- Nonprofit fundraisers

- Authors

- Job seekers

- "Everyone"…

Seriously. *Many* so-called experts say *everyone needs* an elevator speech, all the time, for every situation, from when you run into an old friend in the grocery store to when you're stuck in traffic or in line for a movie. Think about the ridiculousness of that all-inclusive language for a moment.

That means a sleepless stay-at-home mom or dad in the throes of the newborn baby stage—while also juggling the unreasonable demands of a toddler who just smeared toothpaste all over the bathroom wall like finger paint, and simultaneously trying to convince a six-year-old that wearing pink footie pajamas to the swimming pool in July might be a bad idea—should take some time to craft an elevator speech.

Because after all, "everyone" needs it—every time, all the time. That mom may be at a PTA meeting and someone could ask her the question, "What do you do?" She should be prepared, because after all, simply saying what might come to her in the moment, "I have three kids, a dog, and a husband who works two jobs, I volunteer at church, and in my spare time I write articles as a freelancer. I do *a lot,*" somehow isn't going to cut it.

Apparently, even people doing academic research need an elevator speech, as do college graduates without a job but who want to stand out in the sea of job-seekers. According to some schools of higher learning, graduate students need to have an elevator speech prepared when someone asks about their school or graduate program. One school even goes so far as to have crafted an elevator speech for its students and posted it on its Website:

The College University [real name removed to avoid embarrassment over being obnoxious] is nationally known for its groundbreaking research, frequently published faculty, award winning facilities and world renowned alumni. We are ranked fifth in the "Top Schools for Science" list published by List magazine annually, and our team mascot has been named "Best Mascot of the Year" two seasons running by Mascot International...

Yes. Really.

Look at the lunacy of even creating this statement, as if students haven't checked it out previously or as if they chose to attend the school because of its mascot. But what's more, this school even goes so far as to ask students:

Have you ever been asked to opine about your beloved university in a social, networking or other situation? Have you ever been stumped for a really good, quick, concise answer to give them? We can offer you a simple "elevator speech" that provides all the "bullet points" anyone needs to know about our fine institution and why we're so beloved nationally and internationally—all in the time it takes to ride three or four floors on the elevator....

The wording of this statement implies that someone actually expects graduate students working on advanced degrees to take time away from their research and lives to *memorize* this inane marketing drivel and spit it out at someone who asks them where they go to grad school. What student have you ever met would do that? Not even the straight-A student who loves her school, program, department, and faculty would bother memorizing that diatribe.

Sadly, there are many colleges and universities, as well as other corporate and nonprofit organizations that have the same type of pre-fabbed, pre-arranged, pre-programmed "scripts" on their sites. I think we've taken the idea that common sense isn't so common to an extreme when an organization feels it has to provide a scripted elevator speech to give the people associated with it a way to describe what they live every day.

But now, let's delve deeper into the various flaws associated with the traditional elevator speech and, specifically, why it's so ineffective. In my experience over the years, I've identified six specific problems with the elevator speech, and will highlight them for you now:

PROBLEM 1: SPOKEN WORD VERSUS WRITTEN WORD

The phrase in the statement from the public state university that suggests the students use the information elsewhere is key: "It can also be used for grants, proposals, and any other written project requiring a description of our college...."

The challenge is that people are confusing the use of the written word and the use of the spoken word. Put simply: *they are different.* Playwrights and scriptwriters will tell you writing for dialog, even monologue (which is essentially a speech), is vastly different from writing a scene in a novel.

Characters come to life based on the words the playwrights choose and the manner in which they direct the character to speak. You are a character in your own life and in representing yourself personally and as a business professional. The words you choose and the manner in which you choose to share them will make you come to life in a way that represents who you are, your personality, your feelings, your beliefs, and everything about you.

Characters in a novel are also static; they are frozen in time, in place, in the way the author of that novel or play or movie wrote them. They are responding to pre-set, pre-arranged, orchestrated actions and incidents and dialogue that don't exist in the real world.

Even if you feel your life is routine, it isn't. There are hundreds of random moments we experience each day that are completely unlike the random moments of the day before and will never happen again in the same, exact way. So when we respond, it's spontaneously to what is happening live and in person. To try and bend our lives, and in particular our interactions to a "script," is to deny the random spontaneity that makes life...life.

There is an inherent challenge when you sit down to write a script about who you are, with no script-writing experience, no understanding of how to fully communicate your character. That is a major problem with many of the "how to write elevator speech" books and training materials out there today. Going back all the way to Aristotle, scholars have shared the distinctions between the written word and the spoken word in both function and style.[2]

So if the primary purpose of speaking is to build and maintain relationships, the primary purpose for the words you speak when you meet someone should be the same. Therefore, sitting down to write the words you plan to say, will lead you to the path of writing information, and away from building a relationship with a person in the moment, in front of you, with whom you are having a conversation.

PROBLEM 2: ELEVATOR SPEECH = QUICKLY FORGOTTEN

In fact, using an elevator speech is a direct route to quickly being forgotten. Counterintuitive? Not at all. Consider this: when someone is speaking and sharing his or her elevator speech, this means, theoretically, someone else is listening. The listening process is so crucial to a conversation and networking that later I devote an entire chapter to discussing it. For now, it's important to note some challenges uncovered by the research with regard to using an elevator speech and listening.

Various studies have suggested that people can only recall 17.2 percent of the information they just heard on the evening news,[3] meaning that people listening for information actually recall only a small degree of the information they just heard. And it seems to me that what people remember most are those things that are personal to them, meaningful and unrehearsed, not some "canned" version of your biography that's crammed with details like the previous "college campus" example.

We also must take into account that while we like to "think" people we meet at a networking meeting, for example, are hanging on to our every word, the reality is they are most likely being distracted by a number of factors including being hungry or having a headache, other people around them talking, or simply a lack of interest in what we're saying.[4] Ouch, right?

So what the research on listening tells us is that people we meet at a business or other meeting are not likely to remember what we've said at all, let alone details we might choose to share with them through a memorized speech of some kind. Therefore, the elevator speech is a waste of your valuable time because your carefully selected, memorized words will not be remembered.

So what *are* people capable of remembering?

As I was perusing Facebook one evening, a professional speaker colleague of mine was lamenting the fact that an acquaintance had recently introduced her as "the owner of a very large marketing firm." That would be fine, except she is a solo-entrepreneur who offers speaking and consulting that is based from her home. Alone. No big marketing firm. Seems she might be missing the mark on describing herself so people will remember her.

One of the challenges many of my clients have struggled with over the years is what to call themselves and how to introduce themselves. The answer lies in what we want people to remember about us.

The research on listening tells us that people will remember only a tiny fraction of what they've just heard, usually in the neighborhood of about two to three words.[5] That means you're going to be remembered with at most three words, no matter how many words you use to describe yourself.

What's worse than people forgetting how you just described yourself is the fact that they will select and recall only two to three of those words. Clearly, you have a choice: either you can be in control of those two to three words people will remember about you, or you can use a lot of words and hope the two to three words people remember are close to what you want to be remembered for.

In conversation, most people are hard-pressed to remember what *they* just said five minutes ago, let alone what *you* said. After even a brief introduction to you, they'll still only remember about two to three words' worth of detail about you such as, "She's a speaker," or "He's a writer."

Maybe once they get to know you in conversation they'll remember more specific words like "leadership speaker" or "writer of marketing books." Give people those words you want to be remembered by or they'll come up with their own words from your whole, long spiel that doesn't matter to them at all.

To me, the choice seems easy. How about you?

PROBLEM 3: OVERWHELMING

In a recorded video conversation with Bob "The Teacher" Jenkins, Internet and marketing consultant, that I have posted on my blog,[6] we talked about how the elevator speech causes overwhelming feelings for both the listener *and* the speaker. Consider what Bob said in that interview and see how a listener can feel overwhelmed:

- Unsure of the most important details in your elevator speech, an overwhelmed listener will tune out and ignore you instead.

- Knowing the popular current wisdom that says everyone in business "should" have an elevator speech, while listening to you give yours, your listener is overwhelmed with what he should say next and worries that he should really write one soon and should have done it before he came today and when is he ever going to find the time

to get that done and where does he start and…
and…

- Maybe the person could use your services or
  would want to purchase your product, but while
  listening to you extol the fabulousness that is
  you, they become overwhelmed in the possibilities, or confused with the options and choices.
  And you know the old business adage, "A confused mind never buys."

- Sometimes people don't want the most interesting, most exciting, best widget around. It can be
  overwhelming to feel the pressure to live up to
  the expectations of that kind of hype.

- Many people get overwhelmed with clever gim-
  micks and prefer to hear plain language.

- Less obvious are the ways a speaker—that is
  the person delivering the elevator speech—can
  become overwhelmed. Consider:

- As with any speech, no matter how short, you
  could forget your script or a flub a line or
  change a phrasing and become overwhelmed
  with the fact that you didn't get it out perfectly
  and you've worked on this stupid thing so much
  and you can't believe you paid that consultant
  money to tell you how to do it because this is
  just ridiculous…

- Having likely worked with a consultant who wrote it for you or maybe you read a book following the author's steps to write your elevator speech, you could become overwhelmed with your own marketing, thinking to yourself even as you're saying the words out loud, "Is this really me? Can I deliver on this?"

Overwhelming feelings set in for both you and the listener—and then what? Everybody's overwhelmed! And who benefits from that?

PROBLEM 4: MANY PEOPLE DON'T KNOW HOW TO TURN IT OFF

You've probably met people who, at a wedding or another nonprofessional occasion like my physical therapy sessions, when introduced, blurt out their elevator speech and appear to be proud of themselves.

Then, suddenly the conversation just...*stops.* It's awkward. As the awkward silence stretches out we think to ourselves, "Did you just try to sell me something? No? What the heck was all *that* about?" You were simply making polite conversation, but that person had no concept of an appropriate time to talk using "work language" and when to turn it off and just give it a rest. As a result, now you may feel like you need a shower.

Should you always be networking and expanding your network? Absolutely. At every opportunity. Maybe the person sitting at your table at that wedding reception could introduce you to your next best customer or is one herself. If you're not networking, you'll never know. But there is a right way and a wrong way to start a relationship with anyone new—and an elevator speech is not it.

Your network is your entire web of relationships, all of them, no matter where and how you meet people. In his best-selling book *Love Is the Killer App: How to Win Business and Influence Friends,* Tim Sanders explains how, "In the twenty-first century, our success will be based on the people we know. Everyone in our address book is a potential partner for every person we meet. Everyone can fit somewhere in our ever-expanding business universe."[7]

The way to connect with those people? Not with an elevator speech, but by listening to them and, according to Sanders, being willing to share your knowledge, your connections, and your compassion for them as human beings on their unique journey of life.

PROBLEM 5: THE ELEVATOR SPEECH IS NOT CONDUCIVE TO ACTUAL HUMAN CONVERSATION

The purpose of the elevator speech is to have an answer prepared when someone asks you what you do for a living. That way, you're not fumbling for words and missing a golden opportunity. But when you reply to a single person asking that "What do you do" question in friendly conversation with a "speech," you're completely missing the mark—and losing an opportunity.

A conversation is a two-way communication event, not a one-way monologue or presentation, like a public speech. Having a conversation does not entail pre-planning your statements or delivering a forced, rehearsed diatribe. Conversations are spontaneous, random, back and forth and, well, conversational.

Some experts teaching alternative elevator speech models will teach a "conversational method" of elevator speech that follows a template that looks like this:

> You know how [target market] sometimes have a problem with [state problem] and they just get stuck [or other challenge]? Well, I help them [or some other verb] by [state the action of what you do] and they benefit because [state the takeaway for your clients.]

If I was following that format, an example of this template might be:

> You know how some business professionals sometimes worry about what they're going to say and if they should even have an elevator speech? Well, I help them realize they don't even need an elevator speech—not even a conversational one like this—because they just don't work.

Compelling, right?

Well, sort of.

This statement is arguably more conversational. Yet it's also still memorized and not designed to help the person you're speaking to in any way. As you saw discussed with earlier problems, this phraseology simply contains too many words for the other person to remember.

What's more, this type of "you know how" answer has been taught long enough now that when many seasoned business people hear it "in conversation," they immediately recognize it as an elevator speech and begin to turn off and shut down anyway because the deliverer of the speech is in that moment all about herself and not there in authentic conversation with the other person.

You're at a networking function with the express purpose of connecting with others (and if you're there to sell something on the spot you might as well stay home; people will smell that desperation a mile away and steer clear of you). Regurgitating a memorized, canned spiel is not connecting. At all.

In fact, it's quite the opposite.

When networking or sincerely trying to "connect" with someone, your main goal should be to find out if you know someone or something that could be helpful to those you meet. Being helpful is the first step in being memorable. Speaking "at" someone with a pre-planned, canned, "template" speech does not make you helpful in any way.

PROBLEM 6: THE ELEVATOR SPEECH IS NOT AUDIENCE SPECIFIC

When you write any speech, step one always has to be to answer the question, "Who is my audience?" Creating a speech involves knowing your audience—a *group* of people—and understanding them in order to provide value through your words. Technically speaking, talking to one person could be considered an "audience," but delivering a "speech" of any kind to one person is odd at best and either rude, insulting, or obnoxious at worst. (And are any of those adjectives how you want to be remembered?)

Theoretically speaking, if an elevator speech was a good idea, you'd have to prepare it for a specific segment or type of person. However, you have no real idea if the person you're talking to at any given moment is in your niche or target market if you haven't spoken to the person yet.

Sure, you could make an educated guess based on the type of event you may be attending, if it happens to be a networking event, conference, or trade show. Yet the bigger challenge is *anyone* at *any time* could ask you what you do for a living. So then in that moment, you're faced with a choice: to use the elevator speech or not.

If you go with what you've got memorized and the person you're speaking to in no way resembles the person you wrote the speech for, you get that awkward moment of silence. If you write a speech that is "general" to "everyone"—well, that's marketing suicide. So what do you do?

Skip the speech, that's what.

PARTING WORDS

As a professional speaker and communication consultant, I have been asked for years by nervous entrepreneurs and professionals headed to networking meetings and live events about the best way to put together an "elevator speech." And for years I have been telling those same people why they should not have one.

Now you know why!

ENDNOTES

1. Tracy Kidder and Richard Todd, *Good Prose: The Art of Nonfiction* (New York: Random House, 2013).

2. Aristotle, *The Art of Rhetoric,* Book III, Chapter XII.

3. J. Stauffer, R. Frost, W. Rybolt, "The attention factor in recalling network news," Journal of Communication (1983), (33)1, 29-37.

4. K.W. Watson, L.R. Smeltzer, "Barriers to listening: Comparison between students and practitioners," Communication Research Reports 1 (1984), 82-87.

5. Laura Ann Janusik, "Researching listening from the inside out: the relationship between conversational listening span and perceived communicative competence" (2004). Dissertation available at: http://drum.lib.umd.edu/bitstream/1903/1417/1/umi-umd-1429.pdf; accessed June 16, 2014. T.L. Kelly, "Conversational Narcissism in Hyperpersonal Interaction" (Graduate paper, Portland State University, October 1997); http://www.q7.com/~terri/Papers/sp511.htm; accessed June 9, 2014.

6. Visit: http://feliciaslattery.com/blog/communicating-credibility/iced-tea-and-hot-marketing-tips-from-bob-the-teacher-and-felicia-slattery; accessed June 9, 2014. See also, Take Action, Revise Later by Bob Jenkins: http://www.amazon.com/Take-Action-Revise-Later-Business/dp/0982985134; accessed June 9, 2014.

7. Tim Sanders, *Love Is the Killer App: How to Win Business and Influence Friends* (New York: Crown Business, 2002), Chapter 3.

CHAPTER 3

PERSUASIONS AND ARGUMENTS

As you've been reading along so far, you might agree with the common sense part of my argument that essentially asks, "If people neither like to give nor hear the elevator speech, then why is it still around?"

The answer, at least according to those who teach others how to write "effective elevator speeches," is that, when properly crafted *and* deftly delivered, an elevator speech will "work" every time. In what terms these experts use the word "work," is unclear. After all, an elevator speech "working" could mean:

- Having the desired result of being hired or making a sale on the spot (unlikely);

- Having the desired result of the other participant in the conversation say something like, "I know someone who can use your services. I'll refer you!" (again, highly unlikely);

- Having the desired result of the other participant in the conversation ask a follow-up question such as, "How do you do that?" (not quite likely);

- Having the desired result of the other participant in the conversation say something like, "Tell me more." (Really?)

Now, in the case of the last two possibilities when it comes to "working" or not, if your goal is starting a conversation, your elevator speech could fly like a lead balloon, based on the six problems addressed in the previous chapter. That's mainly because the other person in your completely one-sided "conversation about you" will be looking for the nearest exit, bar, or hors d'oeuvre table to get away from you!

Think about that for a second: one elevator ride, two people, and *you* are the only one doing all the talking? And that's supposed to say…*what* about you exactly? If anything's "working" about that scenario, it's the second person coming up with every excuse in the book on how to get out of listening to another word!

WHAT DOES THE DATA SAY?

I would love to provide reams of data on the effectiveness, or ineffectiveness, of the elevator speech. Sadly, there have been very few studies done about elevator speeches or pitches. However, those that *do* exist all lead to one result: professionals spend a lot of time stressing over an elevator speech for exactly *zero return*.

Peter J. Denning and Nicholas Dew, writing on "The Myth of the Elevator Speech"[1] in *Communications of the ACM* (which stands for Association for Computing Machinery—see? there's not a lot of empirical research out there) find, "The data does not support the conventional wisdom that the elevator pitch is a key to success with innovations. The convention is a myth." They also liken the elevator speech to a lottery ticket for those in business, writing "…your pitch is almost certain to be a losing ticket, but you buy it because it is cheap and there is a chance that your 30-second pitch could change everything."

They go on to add that:

> We can now define a pitch as a short conversation that seeks a commitment to listen to an offer conversation…the purpose was to gain a commitment from the other person to have more conversation with you about what you can offer. If you think about the elevator pitch as an offer to discuss how to solve the other person's problem or get a job done for them, you will approach the conversation in a different way from a presentation pitch…. A conversational pitch will get you closer to your idea being adopted.

Research on persuasion, as discussed in depth by Professor Robert B. Cialdini, explains how keeping a message brief, and in plain, simple, and clear language is much more persuasive than longer messages, with flowery language meant to impress a listener.[2]

Research from MIT, compiled in a report entitled "Toward a Social Signaling Framework: Activity and Emphasis in Speech" by William T. Stoltzman, shows there is a high correlation between persuasion, content, and style in a given elevator speech. "What listeners think they are perceiving as good or bad content is actually very heavily influenced by the context (i.e., the delivery). Put another way, your ability to persuade a crowd may have as much to do with your presentation style as your message."[3]

Persuasive speakers talk faster than others and are more charismatic. So what matters more than what you say is how you say it. However, that doesn't mean what you say isn't important, simply that you must also be sure you are speaking in a way that is interesting to your listener.

Further, even at networking meetings where you are there to meet other professionals, you shouldn't expect anyone in the room to immediately hire you on the spot.

That's because business is done differently today. Perhaps back in the not-so-good-ol'-days of the "old boys" network, business-men (weren't they all men back then?) could walk into a breakfast meeting knowing no one and walk out with a new customer. And perhaps not.

Today, however, business success is based squarely on the mutual relationships you are able to build. If you don't believe me, just look at some (not all) of the relationships you'll likely need to foster in order to have a successful company:

- Vendors and suppliers

- Service providers such as accountants, consul-tants, graphic designers, Website managers, etc.

- Clients/customers

- Potential clients/customers

- Colleagues who do what you do

- Colleagues who serve who you serve

- Investors

- Potential investors

- Mastermind partners inside your industry

- Mastermind partners outside your industry

- Accountability partner(s)

- Referral partners

- Employees and staff—both onsite and/or virtual

- Board of directors

- Association leaders and organizers

- Landlord

- Local business community

- News media

- Etc.

Not to mention the people in your personal life who you want to support you including a spouse, partner, children, parents, in-laws, friends, and more. If you're looking to be gainfully employed, you'll have a different set of relationships to foster such as:

- Co-workers in your department

- Co-workers in supporting departments

- Assistant(s)

- People who report to you

- Direct supervisors

- Upper level management

- Customers/clients of your department

- Customers/clients of your organization

- Colleagues in your industry

- Lower-level co-workers such as maintenance and mailroom staff, etc.

As you might imagine, each relationship—each connection, pre-existing, tenuous, or solid—requires a different type of communication. We all know that while everyone deserves respect, there is a different language spoken, often out of necessity, between, for instance, the people you report to and the people who report to you.

Likewise, every industry has its own language, and those of us who "cross pollinate" from one industry to the next, like coaches, consultants, public speakers and salespeople, know how to change hats and speak in the language common to each industry.

To imagine one speech, pitch, or script that could encompass all of the complexity within and without an organization boggles the mind.

ARGUMENT FALLACIES FOR AN ELEVATOR SPEECH

When I was an adjunct instructor of public speaking at several local colleges and universities, one of my favorite chapters to teach was persuasion. Why? Simple: because every student would need persuasive skills throughout his or her life, in a variety of capacities.

For instance, they would need persuasive skills to get a job, get a raise, get a promotion, find a spouse or long-term life partner, and convince people at work and in their personal lives to do all sorts of small *and* big things all the time. Persuasion is a life skill we all need to master to be the most successful we can be.

Unfortunately, when presenting their initial persuasive outlines for their upcoming speeches, many of my students tended to rely on one or more of the most common persuasive fallacies. Helping them understand these fallacies in context of what each wanted to persuade made it easier for the students to avoid the fallacies.

For reference, here are five of the top persuasive fallacies as to why you "need" an elevator speech, each one applied to common arguments in favor of having and using an elevator speech. Underneath each is why I feel such an argument is a flat-out fallacy:

Ad hominem or Attack on the Person Instead of the Argument: "Anyone who tells you that you don't need an elevator speech is a quack and doesn't care about you or your business. They also probably don't like babies or puppies."

Why this is a fallacy: Well, this is an easy one. People like *New York Times* best-selling author Michael Port could hardly be called a "quack," yet in his wildly popular book *Book Yourself Solid,* he clearly advocates *against* using an elevator speech. I also happen to know for a fact that he does care about his clients; and I'll go out on a limb here and say that I'm pretty sure he likes kids and puppies, too.

Post hoc ergo propter hoc or False Cause: "If you have an elevator speech, you'll automatically be able to start a conversation with people about what you do."

Why this is a fallacy: This argument assumes that without an elevator speech you wouldn't be able to start a conversation about what you do which is, of course, totally false. Conversation at business events usually flows easily and naturally, especially *when it doesn't feel forced*. Using an elevator speech does not in and of itself cause conversation and, in fact, it could easily become the lead balloon of a conversation and stop it before it even starts.

Reductio ad absurdum or Reduction of the argument to the absurd: "If you don't have an elevator speech, you might as well not even be running a business because you're not serious about business and you will never become a success anyway."

Why this is a fallacy: Maybe this argument doesn't exactly come out in so many words, but it certainly feels like that to many of my clients who have asked me to help them with their elevator speeches. What's more, it assumes that those who don't have elevator speeches aren't worthy of running a business—or succeeding—both of which are great examples of specious reasoning.

Argumentum ad verecundiam or False Authority Appeal: "You should have an elevator speech because networking and marketing experts say you need one. Studies show they work."

Why this is a fallacy: Excuse the colloquialism, but that's a bunch of malarkey. Whenever you see a person argue that "studies show" one thing or another, look at them askew until they tell you their source. Of course, you could run into a problem of one so-called expert quoting another so-called expert, with neither having any real evidence, so pay attention. If there are no cited studies by an association, corporation, university, or published in a verifiable journal with both valid and reliable statistics included, the argument is likely to be just more hot air.

Argumentum ad populum or Bandwagon Appeal: "Everybody knows you need an elevator speech. Everybody in business has one."

Why this is a fallacy: Like your mother probably asked you when you were a teenager, making typical teenager bad decisions just because your friends did it, "If everybody else was jumping off a bridge because it was supposedly good for business, would you?" Okay, my mother never asked it that way either, but you get the point. Just because "Everybody's doing it" is not a valid reason why you should, too. (And anyone who says so should be regarded with suspicion.)

I'm sure you've heard similar arguments yourself, and hopefully now I've given you a little ammunition to refute them on your own.

ENDNOTES

1. Peter J. Denning and Nicholas Dew, "The Myth of the Elevator Speech," Communications of the ACM, Vol. 55 No. 6 (June 2012), 38-40.

2. Robert B. Cialdini, Ph.D., Influence—The Psychology of Persuasion (New York: HarperBusiness, 2007). See also *Yes!: 50 Scientifically Proven Ways to Be Persuasive* by Noah J. Goldstein, Ph.D., Steve J. Martin, Robert B. Cialdini, Ph.D. (New York: Free Press, 2009).

3. William T. Stoltzman, "Toward a Social Signaling Framework: Activity and Emphasis in Speech," MIT (September 2006). http://hd.media.mit.edu/tech-reports/TR-608.pdf; accessed June 7, 2014.

CHAPTER 4

A NATION OF JOINERS

In 1831, a young substitute judge, 25-year-old French aristocrat Alexis de Tocqueville, visited the United States with fellow prison reformer and French magistrate, 28-year-old Gustave de Beaumont on a commission by the French government to inspect the American prison system. After nine months abroad, they returned home and published a report entitled, *On the Penitentiary System in the United States and Its Application to France.*

However, beyond their study of the American prison system, the young French reformers were interested in learning about the American social and political institutions. They were easily accepted by the wealthy American society class (presumably without an elevator speech) and during their time from May through one of the reportedly most harsh winters in recorded history, had access to speak to Americans of every level and profession, including two presidents and Charles Carroll, the last surviving signer of the Declaration of Independence, who also reportedly did not use an elevator speech.

The result of that trip became one of the most in-depth written discussions and analysis of the United States and a democratic

society. *Democracy in America,* the two-volume book de Tocqueville published in 1835 (Volume I) and 1840 (Volume II), is
still widely discussed even in this century and regarded as one
of the preeminent works on the United States political and social
systems today. In that book, de Tocqueville noted how the United
States of America was, and arguably still is, a nation of joiners
and people who want to connect with each other. De Tocqueville
wrote the following in Volume II, Chapter V, titled, "Of the Use
Which the Americans Make of Public Associations in Civil Life":

> Only those associations that are formed in civil life
> without reference to political objects are here referred
> to. The political associations that exist in the United
> States are only a single feature in the midst of the
> immense assemblage of associations in that country.
> Americans of all ages, all conditions, and all dispo-
> sitions constantly form associations. They have not
> only commercial and manufacturing companies, in
> which all take part, but associations of a thousand
> other kinds, religious, moral, serious, futile, general
> or restricted, enormous or diminutive. The Ameri-
> cans make associations to give entertainments,
> to found seminaries, to build inns, to construct
> churches, to diffuse books, to send missionaries to
> the antipodes; in this manner they found hospitals,
> prisons, and schools. If it is proposed to inculcate
> some truth or to foster some feeling by the encour-
> agement of a great example, they form a society.
> Wherever at the head of some new undertaking you
> see the government in France, or a man of rank in

England, in the United States you will be sure to find an association....

...Thus the most democratic country on the face of the earth is that in which men have, in our time, carried to the highest perfection the art of pursuing in common the object of their common desires and have applied this new science to the greatest number of purposes....[1]

The chapter concludes with the following paragraph:

Among the laws that rule human societies there is one which seems to be more precise and clear than all others. If men are to remain civilized or to become so, the art of associating together must grow and improve in the same ratio in which the equality of conditions is increased.[2]

According to the American Society of Association Executives, in 2009, the most recent year with published statistics, there were 90,908 trade and professional associations in the United States.

Clearly, we are still, almost two hundred years after Alexis de Tocqueville visited the United States, a nation of joiners.

How we got this way was explained in a 1944 journal article by Arthur M. Schlesinger, "Biography of a Nation of Joiners," published in *The American Historical Review*. The United States was founded by people who were fiercely independent. If that leads you to question when we became a nation of joiners, Schlesinger explains:

At first thought it seems paradoxical that a country famed for being individualistic should provide the world's greatest example of joiners. How this came about is the object of this sketch, but the illusion of paradox may be dispelled at once. To Americans individualism has meant, not the individual's independence of other individuals, but his and their freedom from government restraint.[3]

The great joining movement began in colonial days most frequently related to religion and politics/government. After winning independence for the United States, because all coastal land was spoken for, businessmen moved inland, to the other side of the mountains to Western Pennsylvania, New York, Ohio, and beyond. In order to survive, they formed associations to help the government.

In the century before de Tocqueville, one of our founders can be credited with being the father of the American association. During the years 1727-1757, Benjamin Franklin, at the young age of 21, founded his "Junto," a weekly discussion group with twelve like-minded men who shared his passion for learning and conversation. The name Junto itself is derived from the Spanish "to join," which could very well be how the idea of Americans as a nation of joiners began.

Topics of discussion at Franklin's Junto were determined by a series of twenty-four questions Franklin created in order to spark ideas and creativity in its members. According to Franklin's autobiography, he described the conversation and content of discussion as such:

The rules that I drew up required that every member, in his turn, should produce one or more queries on any point of Morals, Politics, or Natural Philosophy, to be discuss'd by the company; and once in three months produce and read an essay of his own writing, on any subject he pleased.[4]

What I find fascinating about the Junto concept is, as we saw in previous chapters, how questions spark conversation and ideas. Here is a list of Franklin's questions for his Junto members, as they were originally presented without being corrected for today's language usage:

- Have you met with any thing in the author you last read, remarkable, or suitable to be communicated to the Junto? particularly in history, morality, poetry, physics, travels, mechanic arts, or other parts of knowledge?

- What new story have you lately heard agreeable for telling in conversation?

- Hath any citizen in your knowledge failed in his business lately, and what have you heard of the cause?

- Have you lately heard of any citizen's thriving well, and by what means?

- Have you lately heard how any present rich man, here or elsewhere, got his estate?

- Do you know of any fellow citizen, who has lately done a worthy action, deserving praise and imitation? or who has committed an error proper for us to be warned against and avoid?

- What unhappy effects of intemperance have you lately observed or heard? of imprudence? of passion? or of any other vice or folly?

- What happy effects of temperance? of prudence? of moderation? or of any other virtue?

- Have you or any of your acquaintance been lately sick or wounded? If so, what remedies were used, and what were their effects?

- Who do you know that are shortly going [on] voyages or journies, if one should have occasion to send by them?

- Do you think of anything at present, in which the Junto may be serviceable to mankind? to their country, to their friends, or to themselves?

- Hath any deserving stranger arrived in town since last meeting, that you heard of? and what have you heard or observed of his character or merits? and whether think you, it lies in the power of the Junto to oblige him, or encourage him as he deserves?

- Do you know of any deserving young beginner lately set up, whom it lies in the power of the Junto any way to encourage?

- Have you lately observed any defect in the laws of your country, of which it would be proper to move the legislature an amendment? Or do you know of any beneficial law that is wanting?

- Have you lately observed any encroachment on the just liberties of the people?

- Hath any body attacked your reputation lately? and what can the Junto do towards securing it?

- Is there any man whose friendship you want, and which the Junto, or any of them, can procure for you?

- Have you lately heard any member's character attacked, and how have you defended it?

- Hath any man injured you, from whom it is in the power of the Junto to procure redress?

- In what manner can the Junto, or any of them, assist you in any of your honourable designs?

- Have you any weighty affair in hand, in which you think the advice of the Junto may be of service?

- What benefits have you lately received from any man not present?

- Is there any difficulty in matters of opinion, of justice, and injustice, which you would gladly have discussed at this time?

- Do you see anything amiss in the present customs or proceedings of the Junto, which might be amended?[5]

In studying Franklin's questions, we can ask similar questions today when meeting people and wanting to spark our own interesting conversation. Let's change a few of Franklin's questions and consider how each might be a good way to open a conversation with a stranger:

- What are your favorite business books and are you reading anything right now? Of course you could also share your own book favorites and great current reads. As I was preparing the content for this book I never lacked fodder for conversation. As long as you are reading, you'll always have something to talk about.

- What is your favorite charity right now? Are you doing anything to support it or taking an active role?

- Is there anyone here you're interested in meeting or who you came in particular to see?

Notice again how it is well-worded questions that bring conversation and connection. When you ask better questions, you start to create connections and develop relationships.

ENDNOTES

1. Alexis de Tocqueville, *Democracy in America*, Volume II, Chapter V, "Of the Use Which the Americans Make of Public Associations in Civil Life," 129-134.

2. Ibid.

3. Arthur M. Schlesinger, "Biography of a Nation of Joiners," published in The American Historical Review (1944), I.

4. Benjamin Franklin, "Citizen Ben: Networker"; http://www.pbs .org/benfranklin/l3_citizen_networker.html; accessed June 7, 2014.

5. Benjamin Franklin, http://www.pbs.org/benfranklin/pop _juntoquestions.html; accessed June 7, 2014.

CHAPTER 5

IT'S ALL ABOUT THE AUDIENCE

In public speaking, we call the people we are speaking to our "audience." In professional communication, we also consider anyone who we prepare any message for an audience, whether that be a live audience—as in speaking from a stage or behind a lectern—or an audience of readers reading a book (hello!), or an audience of viewers watching a video or TV program. Regardless who we're speaking to, our audience includes the people with whom we share our messages and it is *their* interpretation of those messages that matter the most.

When marketing anything, to *anyone,* the first question you need to ask yourself is, "Who does this product or service serve best?" After all, the first part of marketing is the *market.* The people are always the first consideration and when you're making decisions about what to share and how to share it, it's always wise to come back to your first question about the market—the audience, the people.

In understanding the elevator speech and why it *does not work,* going beyond the research and the simple fact that nobody likes the darn thing, here's yet another reason why an elevator speech doesn't make sense: it has to do with understanding your audience.

When you truly understand and know your audience, any speech or book or even conversation can flow simply and organically because you *know who you're talking to*. Via empathy and understanding, you can better imagine their challenges, pain, struggles, and provide solutions and answers to those versus giving some canned, generic speech. Yet, when you don't know who your market is, you're clueless as to who they are and how to help them.

As you meet new people, you have something important to consider: you have no idea about *anything* related to who they are, let alone know if they are in your audience. Case in point: imagine yourself arriving at a networking meeting or conference. As you step into the main reception area for the event, you see a friendly face approaching you to introduce herself.

"Hi," says Mrs. Friendly Face. "I'm Suzy Surprise."

Now, if *all* you know is a person's name and a few other clues such as how she is dressed and the fact she is in the same room, you have no idea who she is and what she's about.

But in marketing we hear all the time, and rightfully so, that we need to *know who our audience is*. We have to think about who they are and how they think, what they value and what's important to them. And of course that's definitely important in a marketing piece or on your Website, where visitors will land and you want them to see your specific message crafted *just for them*.

But here's what's *really* happening when Suzy comes over and shakes your hand: she is an audience. An audience of *one*. And every person is unique and sees the world from his or her own colored glasses.

So let's talk about Suzy. Suzy's wrinkled dress has a little spot of something on the shoulder. And you think maybe she's a poor, single mom. You don't know it, but Suzy's youngest daughter just started her first day of preschool this morning, and she's been pretty sad about the little one leaving the nest for the first time. They had a tearful, long hug goodbye before she headed to this meeting. And even though she is new to her current business, she was a highly successful VP of online marketing in a corporate job before she had her first baby ten years ago, when she quit to be home with her kids. She got a little restless at home and so between baby #2 and #3, she started her own daycare business, which she quickly turned into a budding franchise and sold off for more than a million dollars.

Now she's launching her next business. And you're going to march up to her and tell her you help women in business like her develop their online marketing. What will you look like to *her* with that kind of generic, non-targeted approach? (Don't answer that! It's a rhetorical question!)

The reason your elevator speech won't work on Suzy is that you're not focused on *her;* you're focused on *you* (and maybe her pocketbook). What's more, you lose any opportunity to plug into this amazing woman's network and so many other opportunities that come along with treating people like real, live human beings instead of the next score on your professional dance card.

At that point you might as well have taken out the megaphone, stood in the corner of the room and started yelling, "Buy

My STUFF! Hey YOU! BUY MY STUFF!" Because really...the elevator speech isn't much more effective than that.

IT'S NOT JUST ABOUT YOU: EMBRACING YOUR TARGET AUDIENCE

Here's more evidence that it's not all about you: a study published in the *Journal of Personality and Social Psychology* found that what people think of you is partly due to what mood they are in *when they meet you*.[1] Those in a happy, upbeat, positive mood when you meet are more likely to think of you in a positive way. And for someone who is in a bad mood, well...their first impression of you will tend to be more negative. And that may have nothing to do with you. Maybe they've had a bad day at work, couldn't find close parking, had a fight with their partner, and the dog ruined another pair of shoes. They may never tell you any of these personal things, but you'll be the unlucky recipient of a negative judgment through no fault of your own. Further, if someone happens to be in a good mood, they are more likely to remember more details about you than those who are not.

The obvious advice here is to steer clear of Grumpy McGloomy in the back of the room. However, the sad fact is, most of us learn from an early age to put on a happy face no matter what mood we are truly in. So you may not have any warning that the person you're speaking to is in a bad mood, which will most likely mean an unfavorable opinion of you regardless of what you say and how you say it.

One way to stand out in a positive light, regardless of what mood someone is in when you first meet the person, is to master the ancient art of listening:

THE LISTENING PROCESS

While the listening process at first seems simple, it is actually a complex system involving multiple steps that, unfortunately, is all but ignored in our formal education. In fact, humans spend most of their communication time not in writing, reading, or even speaking (be still my speaking coach's heart!), but in listening.

THE IMPORTANCE OF INTERPERSONAL LISTENING

According to a report by Judi Brownell at Cornell University published in the December 1994 edition of *The Bulletin,* studies have found that employees of major corporations in North America spend about 60 percent of their work day, *every* day, *listening to others,* while some industries point to listening as the most important communication skill needed to advance in their careers. Better listeners tend to excel in the workplace, do well on work teams, and are perceived as strong leaders.

In an article in the *Journal of Personal Selling and Sales Management,* Stephen Castelberry and David Shepherd defined interpersonal listening as the process "by which individuals receive informational messages transmitted by others." Meeting people, whether at work or in your personal life, involves interpersonal listening on a daily basis.

In interpersonal relationships inside the home, wives have complained for decades that their husbands, "Never listen to me!" Yet, as important as listening is to professional and personal success, shockingly little attention is paid to teaching listening skills throughout childhood and even into adulthood.

A quick look at my daughter's elementary school report card shows the typical subjects you'd expect: reading, English, social studies, science, math, technology, art, physical education, handwriting, music, and even conduct—but nowhere is there feedback for "listening." What a missed opportunity. Think how different our personal and professional lives might be if we were as fluent in listening as we were in reading, writing, and arithmetic!

You would think that higher learning might value the fine art of interpersonal listening, right? Wrong again! Most colleges and universities don't even offer a course in listening. However, the good news is that those students who take a communication, speech, or interpersonal class may get at least a chapter about listening.

Yet in terms of the overall population of college students, those numbers of students who are *actually* exposed to listening education in classes are low. Beyond that, just because a student studied a particular skill in college does not necessarily equate to having success with the same skill in "real life."

LISTENING IS COMPLEX

Myths about listening abound. One of the largest misconceptions of listening is that if a person speaks the same language as the speaker and he hears a person's voice, listening has occurred. Physical hearing is only the first step in the process, and without paying attention (step 2) and understanding (step 3), true listening has not occurred. If you've been married for more than twenty minutes, you know hearing does not equate to listening.

My husband has the common ability to be present in the same room as I am, nod his head to acknowledge he has "heard" me, and then almost immediately not have any idea what I just said. He does not remember the meaning behind the sounds that indicate he has to pick up the kids at school tomorrow for whatever reason.

I'll remind him the next day and he'll say, "Oh, I didn't know I was picking the kids up from school today." Right. Because he wasn't *listening*. (He's forgiven every time because I still love him and have learned to text him reminders, but that's for another book J.) Simply hearing sounds does not mean the message will get through any more than nodding one's head is an indication of true understanding.

LISTENING AND THE PROCESS OF COMMUNICATION

Why is listening so complicated? There are a variety of reasons. For one, there is noise all around us. When you look at the transactional model of communication in Chapter 1, which is the common and current modern model of communication, you can clearly see there can be noise at any point in the process, and how it might interrupt the normal flow of any conversation:

Figure 6.1: Transactional Model of Communication

Let's examine this model more closely in a networking situation: "Trish" thinks that she would like to meet and speak with "Brian," the newest member at her regular networking meeting that week. Trish, who is a longtime member of this particular group, has been on vacation and has missed the past two meetings. Trish wants to welcome the newcomer, Brian, to the group. And now the noise ensues in multiple places.

Communication noise for Trish could include her own self talk that includes the fact that her youngest happened to spill his milk and some of it got on the cuff of her blazer that morning, and she didn't have time to change before coming to the meeting. So as she begins to introduce herself, and reaches out to shake Brian's hand, she notices the light stain of milk and is reminded that she probably should go to the store after the meeting and buy some more milk for home. Oh, and while she's there, maybe she could use a loaf of bread, too. Not to mention one of those laundry soap pens for her purse so this never happens again. All this happens in the flash of a moment, and all while Brian is introducing himself with his elevator speech; a speech that she hasn't listened to a word of because of her internal "noise."

In the next moment, as Trish begins to speak, Brian is now left wondering why she didn't respond to his elevator speech the way he wanted her to, but instead just started talking about herself. Did he forget to say something? Maybe he should have worn a tie to this meeting after all. Or maybe her brain is still on vacation and she doesn't get how great he is. Or something else.

So now Brian has his own internal noise. Not to mention the ice machine is near them in this restaurant meeting space, and as they are speaking to each other it's dumping ice, plus the drone of other conversations floating around the room, not to mention the fact that Trish's soft voice is hard to hear anyway. Immediately after that, Brian's text message alert goes off in his pocket, making him wonder who that could be. Standing behind Brian is Christine, trying to get Trish's attention.

Meanwhile, physical noise from the environment is now infecting the conversation. With all of the internal noise and external noise in every communication situation, it's a wonder any communication takes place!

Ah, but you see, communication *does* take place, and often those messages have nothing to do with listening at all. The messages may not be the messages we intend to send, but that stain on Trish's cuff could send a message that she doesn't pay attention to detail, although the truth is she is hyper-aware of details and that drop of milk is driving her batty. Brian's text message—and his immediate insistence on reaching for his phone—could send the message that he's rude and too focused on what is happening outside the room rather than with the people in front of him. What's really happening is he's waiting on news about some minor outpatient surgery one of his retired parents in Florida is having that morning.

COMMUNICATION, LISTENING, AND BUSINESS

When you realize that listening is a process that involves not only hearing another person's voice, but also paying attention to and understanding the spoken words, you can see how the landscape is fraught with potential problems in any business situation. Add to that the internal and external noise that surrounds nearly any event and listening isn't the only process involved in communication in business. For a moment, let's continue to look at the impact of how—and how well—we can listen.

Even when listening for information being transmitted by others, with all the internal and external noise going on around you, as mentioned previously, people can only recall 17.2 percent of the information they just heard on the evening news. And that's not interacting with another person, but watching TV. So if people are most likely going to remember just a small percentage of our conversation, it should at the very least *be meaningful to them.*

Far more than the words we say, what most people will remember is their impression of us, which is based in large part on what we choose to say combined with the nonverbal messages we send simultaneously. In the next section we'll discuss the importance of nonverbal communication in greater detail, but for now, let's simply look at the words we choose by way of leaving an impression.

According to the *Journal of Personality and Social Psychology*,[2] research has shown that the words you choose will leave an impression, and that impression is formed subconsciously. No matter what the rest of the conversation sounded like, the person to whom you are speaking will make judgments about who you are based on what you say and, what's more, will form those judgments *without even realizing why.*

We also must take into account that while we like to *think* people we meet at a networking meeting, for example, are hanging on our every word, the reality is they are most likely being distracted by a number of factors completely outside our control, including:

- Being hungry;

- Recently receiving bad news;

- Having a headache;

- Twelve chores to do when they get home that night;

- Other people around them talking;

- Background noise;

- Simply not being interested enough in what we're saying to give us their full attention...

But instead of looking at the first words you say to a person as being like a heat-seeking missile designed to separate them from their money, think instead about how you can truly create a connection with this person.

How do you do that? By listening. So now, instead of the conversation being about you, you start to make it about them. You do this by asking questions and then—shocker, I know—actually *paying attention to the answers.*

Research has shown that the two most important interpersonal variables in sales success are empathy and listening skills.[3] That's likely because, in order to serve anyone, you have to first understand their needs and their wants.

But wait, don't go off thinking you can ask any of those stupid, jerky marketing questions and call it "empathy," or nod your head until the other person's mouth starts moving and call it "listening skills." Case in point: I once saw a person who called himself a professional speaker proudly admit in a forum that he likes to start all *his* speeches with the attention-getting question: "Who wants to make more money?!" And he says he keeps on berating the poor audience with that until they finally raise their hands in compliance.

Yes, really. Talk about a terrible introduction!

Okay, okay, so no asking stupid, "marketing-driven" leading questions that have only one obvious and ridiculous answer. Also, don't ask the tired "What keeps you up at night" question. Every hack salesperson who's taken some 1980s version of training in "How to Ask Questions" asks that.

But what happens when you're the person who has to speak first? I remember one time early in my career I was at a networking event and was locked in a standoff with someone who wanted to be the one who was interested. Neither one of us wanted to "go first," so there we were like teenagers in love on the phone not wanting to hang up, "No, *you* go first." "No *you* go."

So it's inevitable that at some point you will be the one who has to go first. Typically you'll get asked, "What do you do?" And in true politician style you are *not* going to answer that question.

Instead, you will answer the question that you'd really like to answer. Remember, just because someone asks a literal question doesn't mean they actually want an answer to that question, or that you're bound to give it to them.

Tell the story you want to tell by answering the question you want to drive the conversation, which is: "How did you get started in your business?" And then you're going to tell a story.

Your story should include how long you've been in your chosen field and also who you serve. And your story should include a client's success story so it's obvious what you do, who you do it for, and what the benefits are to them.

Or you can answer the question: "What is the most exciting thing you have going on in your business right now?" The dialogue around this particular question might go something like this:

"Hi Felicia. I'm Suzy. I haven't seen you at this event before. What do you do?"

And, rather than answer her literal question, I'd respond to the question I'd much rather answer by saying, "Hi Suzy. Well, actually right now I'm working on my next book. I've been a *speech coach* [those are the two words she's going to remember] for years and have always had clients who've been through my Signature Speech course asking me to teach them how to do these horrible 'what do you do' speeches everybody hates, right? So I finally decided to write a book about why I won't teach them, because really it's about connecting with another person. Don't you think that's better anyway?"

And now we're having a conversation where I will soon be able to ask Suzy what got her started doing what she's doing and we're off to the races soon laughing and creating a true connection that will be authentic, organic, and memorable.

CREATING A LASTING IMPRESSION

How many people who verbally vomited their elevator speeches onto you, even in a perfectly polished, well-rehearsed manner, did you remember a week later because of their elevator speech? How many is that again? Zero? That's what I thought.

You're not alone. Research performed by Princeton psychologists Janine Willis and Alexander Todorov and later published in the July 2012 issue of *Psychological Science* in their article "First Impressions," reveals that you have the time it takes to blink an eye—that is, 1/10th of a second—before someone has made a judgment about your attractiveness, likability, competence, trustworthiness, and aggressiveness.

Therefore, no matter *what* you say, the first impression is made by a variety of non-verbal messages including your clothing, shoes, jewelry, watch, women's makeup, eye contact, whether or not you smile, your posture, and even physical facial characteristics.

Parting Words

As a professional speaker and communication consultant, I have been asked for years by nervous entrepreneurs and professionals headed to networking meetings and live events about the best way to put together an "elevator speech." It happened again yesterday as I'm writing this. And for years I have been telling those same people why they should not have one: They. Just. Don't. Work.

Stop feeling guilty that you don't have an elevator speech. Stop getting anxious when you know people are going to ask you what you do. Or worse—stop avoiding going to places where you will meet people out of fear they'll ask you what you do and you don't think you have an answer that is a perfectly polished elevator speech. Just. Stop. It.

It's okay. Forget about all you've learned about elevator speeches, trust your intuition—trust me—and give yourself over to the possibility that maybe there is a better way of doing things.

What's truly important is connecting with people, meeting new folks, and seeking to serve those you meet as best you can out of respect for their humanity and yours.

Keep reading and you'll get the simple solution in Part Two.

Endnotes

1. Joseph P. Forgas, Gordon H. Bower, *Journal of Personality and Social Psychology*, Vol. 53(1) (July 1987), 53-60.

2. John A. Bargh and Paula Pietromonaco, "Automatic information processing and social perception: The influence of trait information presented outside of conscious awareness on impression formation," Journal of Personality and Social Psychology, Vol. 43(3) (September 1982), 437-449.

3. Michelle Skinner, "Listening"; http://www.stfrancis.edu/content/ ba/ghkickul/stuwebs/btopics/works/listening.htm; accessed June 7, 2014.

PART TWO

KILL THE ELEVATOR SPEECH ONCE AND FOR ALL

CHAPTER 6

INSTEAD OF THE ELEVATOR SPEECH

> You must have a good time meeting people if you expect
> them to have a good time meeting you. —DALE CARNEGIE

The following vignette was recently posted on the Facebook wall
of actual, real-life venture capitalist and serial successful entrepreneur Com Mirza:

> I've been asked many times what my profession is.
> Even though my whole life is online and clearly vis-
> ible, I still get asked, "So what do you do?" ...My
> response is always, "I'm a full time dream chaser." To
> which most people smile, giggle, and then wonder if
> that really is some kind of occupation. ...Yes friends
> it is a full time occupation, and a very difficult but
> rewarding one to pursue in life....

So there you have it: even the venture capitalist guy who gets
pitched with elevator speeches regularly does not have one himself. And yet what does he do? Rather than shut down potential

dreamers like himself, he encourages them, even inspires them to smile, giggle, and best of all... *wonder*. It may not be a pitch, but it certainly is memorable. And no, you don't have to be so pithy and creative with your reply. However, if you look at his response it certainly fits the two to three word easy-to-remember description: "dream chaser."

And that's where the best connections start.

A LESSON IN EMPATHY

As we begin our discussion around alternatives to the elevator speech, the first place to start is with empathy. In other words, seek to be more *interested* than *interesting*. Yes, I know that sounds counterintuitive to all we've been taught, but read it again: more *interested* than *interesting*.

Empathy starts, and ends, with the other person. It's not a sacrifice if you truly care. And caring is the ground floor on which all empathy begins.

From Merriam-Webster.com, empathy is defined as:

1. The imaginative projection of a subjective state into an object so that the object appears to be infused with it;

2. The action of understanding, being aware of, being sensitive to, and vicariously experiencing the feelings, thoughts, and experience of another [my italics] of either the past or present without having the feelings, thoughts, and experience fully communicated in an objectively explicit manner; also : the capacity for empathy.

Put more plainly, empathy means having the ability to step into another person's shoes and feel what he or she feels. I cannot stress enough how important that is when creating an alternative to the elevator speech.

In the business of simply being a person, empathy is one of the most important interpersonal communication skills you can have. On a more global scale, the lack of empathy in business has been blamed by authors Samuel Michael Natale and Sebastian A. Sora in a July 2010 article in the *Journal of Business Ethics* for nothing short of the "economic collapse in business and government." Further, according to a May 15, 2012, article written on the *Harvard Business Review Network* of blogs, James Allworth believes that the most important lesson his alma mater Harvard Business School teaches is empathy. That's worth repeating: the *most* important lesson Harvard *Business* School teaches is empathy; not statistics, not economics, not finance, but empathy.

On a practical level, empathy is about making a true connection with another human being in a way that is unlike any other. When looking at the elevator speech, consider what the other person is feeling in the moment you dive into your well-rehearsed diatribe about how cool you think you are and how you help people.

Trust me, that other person *is* having an internal dialogue, and if what you're saying doesn't include a little—or hopefully a lot of—empathy than that discussion they're having inside their head isn't about how to reward or do business with you, but how to get away from you.

We are all usually busy. We are all occasionally tired. We are all worried and anxious, or happy and hopeful, or a combination of all of the above, and the last thing we need is to be pitched at, "speeched" or preached to in 30 seconds or less. What we want is a connection, some consideration as to how we're feeling, and trust us, we'll give it right back. Maybe not right away, but certainly at some point. That is the power of empathy, and the reason why listening is so much more important than speaking when you have less than a minute to communicate.

REDISCOVERING EMPATHY

Remember, on a purely relationship level, one of our greatest human needs is to feel like someone understands us and "gets us." This starts from childhood, when our biggest satisfaction comes from being accepted by our parents, family, friends, class-mates, peers, buddies, BFFs, etc. Those are our warmest, fondest, and most rewarding memories and emotions. We get that feeling when someone else listens to us and takes an interest in who we are. In that moment, we feel special.

Empathy can do that. And the best part is this isn't some foreign language or unattainable skill. In fact, empathy is a skill we are born with. Here's proof: if you've ever been in a quiet church service when suddenly one baby begins to cry, only to be joined by most of the other babies in the congregation that day, you've experienced one of the earliest examples of inborn human empathy.

There likely was something happening with the first baby to initiate her crying, maybe a wet diaper, hungry belly, or any number of reasons babies cry. The rest of the babies in the room heard the first cries, which therefore triggered the avalanche of tears and reactions of empathy.

As babies grow, they unfortunately learn the culture of a society that does not necessarily value empathy. As babies, their parents are focusing on whether Junior said "Mama" or "Dada" first, and soon after more language acquisition. As they become toddlers, they learn to experience the physical world around them through walking and later running.

Toddlers and preschoolers are taught basic manners: "Excuse me," "Please," "Thank you" and "You're welcome." And then school age hits. Soon there is reading, writing, math, social studies, and science to discover along with after-school activities.

Subtly, over time and much reinforcement, kids learn to be less empathetic—and more competitive—in Little League, soccer, and other after-school sports. Then social aspects start to come into play: girls begin to notice boys and vice versa.

In all that time, for the most part, there is no one institution responsible for teaching children more complex interpersonal communication skills. Schools are responsible for only so much. Families and parents are busy, and they themselves have no training in expanding empathy, so how can we expect parents to teach their children what they do not know themselves?

As an instructor of many communication courses, including interpersonal communication for more than a decade at various colleges and universities, I have firsthand experience of working with college students who have little knowledge of or experience in living an empathetic life.

Far too many are out for number one, and have no appreciation for, or expectation of, empathy for or from their fellow students. They sadly tend to be very much focused on "number one." Naturally, teaching them empathy is easier said than done. But it starts—in a classroom as well as a boardroom or, yes, even on an elevator—with simply being interested in what the other person is doing, saying, and how they're living.

Trust me, if you make a conversation about them, you will make it about you because they will tell you what you need to know. Here are three simple questions that will help you not just express an interest in other human beings, but also begin to connect with them on a more personal level:

1. How did you get started (doing what you do)?

2. What do you love most (about what you do)?

3. What's the most exciting thing you have happening (in your life/job) right now?

What is the common denominator in those three questions? Look closely and you'll see that it's one simple word—*you*. It's the polar opposite of most elevator speeches, which sound more like:

1. This is how I got started (doing what I do)!

2. This is what I love the most (about what I do)!

3. Here is the most exciting thing I have happening (in my life/job) right now!

Not only are these not even questions, but they're so totally turnoffs it was hard to write them with a straight face. But revisit the first "you" list and look at how valuable "you" questions can be. That is, if you choose to ask them.

THIS SOLUTION WORKS

While developing the content for this book, I attended many networking meetings in order to observe others' interactions, talk to others, and use some trigger phrases to see what answers and reactions I'd receive. Call it my "field study." One such event was on a cold January evening, at a networking event that was the first of the year for the Greater Naperville Networking group, which boasts about 4,500 members on its LinkedIn group.

I thought to myself, *If there's any meeting destined to have a lot of attendees, it's this one.* With so many business people making the New Year's resolutions to "Get more business" or "Meet more people" or simply, "Get away from the computer more often," January events tend to be crowded with wide-eyed opportunists and leaf-turners ready to take on the world.

I wanted to be in the thick of it.

We were crowded in like little soldier ants together in the meeting area, a small-ish bar on one side of a restaurant on a Tuesday night. By this point I'd written much of this book, but wanted to test my alternatives to the elevator speech once again. And it happened, in textbook form.

There we were, balancing our beverages and winter gloves in one hand, ready to shake hands with the other, when I was thrust by the crowd into the midst of two women. They had barely been talking when I happened along. I smiled, glanced at their nametags and with a little laugh said, "Well hi! I guess I'm here!" To which one of the women predictably said to me, "Looks that way! So, what do you do?" I told them both I was writing this book, and the obvious question about what should someone say if not an elevator speech came immediately, as it always does. So

I said, "How about instead of asking you what you do, Barbara, tell me this: how did you get started doing what you do today?" Her eyes lit up like a kid at Christmas seeing her gifts under the tree for the first time. It was as if no one had ever asked her that question. She was so excited to tell me all about how she got started and how she arrived at where she was today. And so was Janice, the second woman, who could barely wait her turn to tell me her story.

Both women were thrilled to be able to talk about themselves and share something neither had expected to talk about that evening. Barbara said, "You know, I will *never* use an elevator speech or ask someone what they do ever again. This way is just too much fun!" She asked for my card and if she could stay in touch with me on LinkedIn because she wanted to know when the book would be out. Smiles and happy moments shared. Connection made.

MEETING OPPORTUNITIES WITH MORE EMPATHY

Before the advent of the Internet as we know it today, with all its myriad ways to communicate, leaving the house was truly the only way to meet new people, unless you had a dinner party at your own home and a guest you invited brought a "plus one." Think about that for a moment: you had to get up, get dressed, be presentable, be social, and go out to meet other living people *in person!* I do have to stress that last bit because for an entire generation of young readers, this is ancient history!

Now, wherever you like to hang out online, you can meet new people, easily and effortlessly. There's Twitter, Facebook, LinkedIn, Google Plus, Pinterest, and Quora, just to name a few sites where people interact with each other, often in meaningful ways, 24 hours a day, seven days a week, 365 days a year.

And even before the current crop of social Websites, there was Ryze and Yahoo Groups, and various forums for every interest under the sun. Before those, there were Usenet conversation groups, which often centered on those with some technical savvy.

However, even with the earliest options to communicate and meet people electronically, that only takes us back to 1980. For me, and probably for you, too, that's well within our lifetime. That means that in just a short period of time, technological communications have come a long way; and of course since the early 2000s, you could even carry all these ways with you in your pocket or purse on your smart phone, including the more personal options of Skype and Face Time!

So why even bother to leave the house today when you can instantly and easily connect with a world full of people all interested in the same topics you are? Many of whom are possible profitable business connections? You can be so much more productive online and even using the phone. There really isn't a reason to get out of the house at all.

Or…is there? (And that's a trick question; of *course* there is!)

According to a 2009 *Forbes* Insights survey of more than 750 business executives, *eight out of ten* respondents said they prefer in-person, face-to-face meetings to technology-enabled ones. Those executives surveyed that prefer face-to-face meetings explained their preference by citing how in-person meetings build stronger, more meaningful relationships (85%), the ability to "read" another person (77%), and greater social interaction (75%). Respondents further noted that face-to-face meetings are best for persuasion, leadership, engagement, accountability, and decision-making.[1]

Further, when meeting new people online, you can never be sure who is at the other end of that electronic communication. The media is ripe with stories of scam artists taking advantage of everyone from lonely-hearts women and even famous former college football player Manti Te'o, who fell for an Internet ruse of a faked girlfriend—who had a fake death—to business scams and even scammers in my own professional speaking industry. (I wrote an in-depth account of one of the more obnoxious ones on my blog.[2])

Social media is *full* of scammers trying to take advantage of people. In my "other" inbox right now on Facebook, there are likely hundreds of messages that read exactly like this (not edited for spelling or grammar):

> Hello,
>
> Charming Angel,how are you doing? i was going through face book when i came across your profile picture and your beautiful smile caught my attention, it seems to me as if you are like the sun that brightens the whole world, and a star that beautify the sky. i will appreciate if you will let both of us swim in the ocean of love and joy to see where it will lead us to,i will also love to know if you can give me the chance to come close to you so that we both can swim in the ocean of love.thanks and am looking forward to hear from you soon.
>
> Love,
>
> Mario.

I don't think you need to be a relationship expert—or even a grammar expert—to sense that the message is obviously a scam of some kind waiting to happen.

But what about the less obvious scams on social media? There are ads down the page promising to tell you "How to build a 10 hour/week, $50,000/month business!" I mean, those *must* be legit, right?! Beyond the obvious scams there are more insidious scams being perpetrated by what look like real people on all sorts of social media outlets.

Yet at a face-to-face event, no Nigerian scammer could ever pretend to be a lottery official in the UK, or try to hire you for a fake speaking gig at a real (and unsuspecting) church asking for several thousand dollars for a "work permit" so you can speak there.

The benefits of face-to-face meetings are clear:

Less room for interpretation. Let's face it: some of us just do better in person. How often has our silly sarcasm, dry wit, or brilliant "snark" gone unappreciated or worse, misunderstood, in a text message, tweet, Facebook comment, networking forum, or message board? In person, you can feel free to be yourself, and encourage others to do the same.

Engaged "Malarkey Meter." One thing I like about in-person exchanges is that when my "malarkey meter" goes off, the one where it's clear someone is selling a bunch of hot air, I'm free to disengage much more quickly than in an online scenario where I can't hear the smarmy tone someone is using.

Make a lasting impression. I tend to be a visual learner and when making connections, it's not just what someone says, but how they look or even act that sticks with me the most. That's almost impossible to get online. In fact, those nonverbal messages are so powerful that they carry much of the meaning of yours and all our messages.

Listen with all your senses. Finally, it's so much easier to "read" someone in person than it is online or even via text or email. Watching their body language, hearing their tone, sensing their enthusiasm, or lack thereof, is so telling; and I'm sure you would agree these are cues that can't be easily masked or faked in person.

So now that we're clear on why face-to-face is preferable to voice, to text, or any other online or technological equivalent, let's look at some strategies for in-person success:

STRATEGIES FOR FACE-TO-FACE NETWORKING SUCCESS

When you do go to a meeting and decide to enter the brave new world where you don't need an "elevator speech" to connect with new people, how can you create a connection with a stranger? How can you focus purely on them, be empathetic, and still get what you want? The following are *seven clear strategies for face-to-face networking success:*

1. *Be Detached from Any Possible Outcome*

When you attend a meeting, be open to the possibilities that might unfold at the meeting and the people you will meet, but not so tied into them that you are instantly disappointed when things don't go your away. Instead, detach yourself from any possible outcome. It's so much more fun to attend a meeting when you look at it as a way to experience other people, and an amazing array of possibilities, rather than to merely "get something" from them.

2. *Make a Nonverbal Impression*

Smile, make eye contact, and pay attention to your nonverbal messages. Far from being secondary, nonverbal communication is the primary way people gather information when they make their first impressions of you. Keep in mind the basics—easy smile, open face, natural eye contact—and you'll be well on your way to creating a positive and memorable connection.

3. *Focus on the Person, Not the Outcome*

In the spring of 2010, I had the honor to meet and share the stage with the amazing, late, great motivational speaker and author Zig Ziglar. In fact, I like to joke that he "opened for me" because he spoke just before I did in the line-up! Before we were both on stage, however, I had the opportunity to sit with Zig and speak with him for a few minutes. As I often do when I'm speaking at events, I save the front of the room seats for the attendees and slide into the back row. As a result of that decision, on the day one of my speaking idols walked into the room, I was one of the first to see him. I greeted him as he entered and welcomed him to the event, introduced myself and told him it was my honor to meet him.

He sat down on a chair next to me and we started to chat. It wasn't more than a minute or two until more and more people in the room realized he'd arrived and they began lining up behind me to have their chance to speak with him. But for all that commotion, Zig didn't pay any attention to them. He was 100 percent focused on me, asking me questions and sharing with me some of his much-loved Zig-wisdom—live and in person! It was one of the most important lessons of my life.

Zig Ziglar was legendary for his ability to shut out all distractions around him and focus solely on the person he was speaking to. Every person who had the joy of experiencing such uninterrupted attention felt how special it was. You can make others feel special, too, just by giving them your full attention and not looking around the room, at your watch, or (gasp!) looking at your smart phone every five seconds. (Trust me, Facebook can wait.)

4. Have an Agenda

Be clear and focused about why you're there. When you go to any meeting, think about why you are choosing to spend your valuable time doing that rather than any of the other 57 things on your to-do list you could be doing instead.

Make it specific. Your agenda should *not* be to make sales or identify prospects, but rather to find a plumber for your neighbor who complained that his sink got stopped up for the third time this year. Or your agenda could include taking a photo with the person who arranged the meeting to thank him or her publicly later on social media for his or her hard work with congratulations on a successful event. Or something else related to connecting with people, not finding prospects, landing a sale, or leaving with more money in your pocket. The most interesting thing is, these things could happen, but those prospects and sales will come out of an authentic connection with another human being rather than any kind of specific scheme to force it to happen.

5. Have No Ulterior Motives

When you meet people and offer something of value to them, do so willingly and freely with no strings attached. Not only will it feel better and more liberating than always, always, always asking for—or pitching—something, but it will actually be more effective in the long run because you will be free to simply be present and communicate. How would that feel? Find out when you try this simple strategy. (And then let me know how it goes!)

6. *Don't Expect Anything from Anyone*

The world doesn't owe you a thing and neither does anyone you meet. The minute you start making demands, real or implied, not only do you lose your "empathy" card but you lose all connection with the other person.

7. *Be More Interested than Interesting*

This is, of course, tried and true advice, but important enough to mention again here. You already know all about you. Seek to learn more about another person and be willing to dig a little deeper. In this book you'll find a few questions to help you learn more about someone else and get a conversation started. In fact, nonverbal communication is another important reason for being face-to-face; you simply can't get a sense for someone's body language on the Web.

PARTING WORDS

As you can see, empathy is a firm guide through the waters of face-to-face meetings. It will help you stay focused, stay clear, and stay centered on the other person so that true communication happens more often than not.

Speaking of conversation, our next chapter is all about the flow.

ENDNOTES

1. Jeff Koyen, report writer, and Brenna Sniderman, survey manager, Forbes Insights, "Business Meetings: The Case for Face-to-Face"; http://images.forbes.com/forbesinsights/ StudyPDFs/Business_Meetings_FaceToFace.pdf; accessed June 7, 2014.

2. You can read what I wrote at http://feliciaslattery.com/blog/ public-speaking/speakers-beware-avoid-the-scammers/.

CHAPTER 7

MASTERING THE FLOW OF CONVERSATION

Conversations are a two-way street. When you meet people at a networking event, family gathering, or other occasion, there is a bit of a dance that takes place. As some people are better dancers than others, some conversationalists are better than others. The good news is, just like the B-list stars on "Dancing with the Stars" TV competition can learn to be better dancers week after week, anyone can learn to be a better conversationalist with some training and practice. The training is in this chapter. The practice is up to you!

BOB BURG'S 10 FEEL-GOOD QUESTIONS

As you move to break away from the elevator speech, both on the giving and receiving end, I want to share with you Bob Burg's trademarked 10 Feel-Good Questions.[1] He is the author of *Endless Referrals*, *Adversaries into Allies*, and co-author of the *Go-Giver* series of books.

1. "How did you get your start in the widget business?"

2. "What do you enjoy most about your profession?"

3. "What separates you and your company from the competition?"

4. "What advice would you give someone just starting in the widget business?"

5. "What one thing would you do with your business if you knew you could not fail?"

6. "What significant changes have you seen take place in your profession through the years?"

7. "What do you see as the coming trends in the widget business?"

8. "Describe the strangest or funniest incident you've experienced in your business?"

9. "What ways have you found to be the most effective for promoting your business?"

10. "What one sentence would you like people to use in describing the way you do business?"

Bob makes an important point about these questions. He suggests that you only ask two or three of these questions during any one conversation. Otherwise you'll come across like an investigative reporter. But let's not stop there. Here is Bob's "One 'Key' Question That Will Set You Apart From Everyone Else": *"How can I know if someone I'm speaking to is a good prospect for you?"*

Before I met Bob, I was inherently using many of these questions in my networking leading me closer and closer toward empathy with each answer. What I've found makes for the best connections is that I also amend or personalize them each time, have added several of my own over the years, switch them in and out of rotation, etc. As with any advice—Zig Ziglar's, Bob's, or mine—the goal should always be to personalize, not memorize.

PROS AND CONS OF COCKTAIL CONVERSATION

When I've met people at various networking events and meetings, I've always been innately curious about them and their stories. One of the things I particularly enjoy about multi-day events that take place out of town where all the speakers and attendees are staying at the same hotel is the ability to sit down with people and get to know them better in a more casual, less "official" context. This usually occurs over meals, often after hours, usually in or near the lounge, otherwise known as "the bar."

In this informal setting, people traditionally unwind more, express themselves more, and just generally loosen up and show you more of who they are, making it easier for you to empathize and communicate with them.

Now, here's a caveat to anyone doing any kind of business networking that involves a bar, especially at a multi-day event where "heading home" for the evening means hopping on the elevator to return to your hotel room. If you choose to imbibe alcoholic beverages of any kind, know your limits and know when to stop. No, you're not driving home. Yes, you can let your hair down and "relax." But no matter how friendly you are with the people there, not *all* of them are personal friends beyond work, and none of them should see you stupid, sloppy drunk. Even if it seems to you like "everybody's drunk, so who cares"?

Don't start with those lame old excuses about how having a cocktail, beer, or glass of wine helps you relax and therefore helps the conversation to flow better. Grow up. If you need a drink to relax, you need more than a book. Learn how to relax without the aid of chemicals. Take a deep breath. Close your eyes for a moment and meditate or say a prayer for peace. Get professional help if you need it.

Just do not get drunk, "buzzed," or "tipsy," no matter how "funny" or "clever" you feel when you are in that state. At some point, likely sooner than later, you'll embarrass yourself and people will remember the wrong thing about you. Even if "everyone else" is drinking heavily or drunk, it is still a mistake to allow yourself to fall into the trap of losing control. Because the truth is *not* everyone else is drinking and there are people who will remember drunk, stupid you instead of the brilliant, beautiful you.

Having said that, connecting with people over a cocktail, beer, or glass of wine is a classic way to be in an informal environment. Maybe the TV will be on and you can talk about sports, the weather, or the news of the day. That's a fine way to connect with someone else as you also learn their interests. Enjoy your beverage of choice. Just be careful about how much of it you enjoy.

THREE MORE QUESTIONS FOR MINING EMPATHY GOLD

We've already discussed the only question you need remember to ask someone to invite conversation: "How did you get started?" But if you want to expand your question repertoire, I offer three stimulating alternate questions.

1. *"What's your favorite part of what you do for a living?"*

When you ask someone to talk about his favorite anything, he will immediately smile and think about something positive. We've already mentioned how a person will make his impression of you based in part on the mood he is in when you meet. When you ask a question that invokes a smile and a happy "feel good" thought, whatever his mood was before you asked becomes elevated because you just asked him to talk about something he enjoys.

Unless, of course, you have the misfortune of speaking to a person who hates every part of his work, in which case this strategy could potentially backfire. (However, let it be noted that this type of person is generally not the best connection to make at a networking event in the first place!)

Use your best judgment in the situation before deciding to ask this question, knowing that most of the time you'll get a favorable and positive response. You will also discover a bit about the person's personality and get a few clues as to what kinds of work-related activities he enjoys, which may lead to more questions and often leads to further discussion—a real "win-win" in my book.

2. *"What is the most frequently asked question you get about what you do and how do you usually reply?"*

This question is a bit more analytical, and is a good one because once again, you'll get the person talking about her work—which is usually a positive, or at least emotional, thing. This should be an easy question for anyone to answer because we all get the same handful of questions over and over again about what we do.

For instance, when I tell people I'm a professional speaker, they will inevitably say things like, "How do you get up there like that? I could never do anything like that!" or "I *love* speaking! How did you get started doing that?" (aha—there's our magic question!), or "What kinds of things do you speak about?"

In any of these cases, the result is the same: immediately, conversation is off and running. And that's exactly what you want. Finally, when you ask for the other person's frequently asked question and she replies, you could say, if it's true, "I've always wondered about that, too."

3. *"Tell me about your best, most amazing dream client you've ever worked with."*

People love this question because they get to present a case study of someone they helped. You instantly make them the hero of their own story. You also get to hear who their ideal client is, what problem the ideal client was confronted with, and how the problem was solved. This allows you to quickly search through your mental database for someone you know like that in order for you to refer them.

I've actually asked this question and then in the same meeting said, "Oh! Did you meet Barbara Jones over there yet tonight? She was just telling me she was looking for exactly that!" And I will bring the two together and introduce them on the spot. I will stay in the conversation only as long as it takes to facilitate the introduction and get past any awkward moments and then step back, excusing myself to the appetizer table for example, to let the magic unfold. Once you've done this a time or two, you get to know what real networking is like and why communication is so powerful.

After all, the more often you connect others, the greater the odds of you being the one a business "matchmaker" pulls over and introduces to a connection that will solve a problem or offer a solution.

BEWARE THE CONVERSATION HOG: THE ART OF BUSINESS CONVERSATION

We've all met people who are conversation hogs. Most of us can point to someone in our close circle of friends or family members who is a conversation hog. What does it mean to be a conversation hog? Simple: in every single interaction and conversation—and I do mean every single one, without exception—this particular person finds a way to turn it back to him. After a while, the unwitting listener in the one-sided "conversation" feels alienated and like they do not matter, whereas the conversation hog simply feels as though he is just making conversation.

Conversation hogs don't get it.

Conversation with others is an art. When you add into the equation the fact that at a business networking function you may not know the other person at all, that art becomes elevated because now you're communicating with a total stranger with no cues to go by except those you pick up yourself. You don't know their attitudes, habits, values…or anything to start with.

And you can't pick up clues when you're the only one doing the talking. That's why questions help. A good question will open up a conversation and get things flowing like a lock on a dam. Open it with a question, particularly one of the open-ended, "feel good" questions I've shared with you, and watch how easily things flow from that point on. Yet when you're with a conversation hog, that flow can quickly become a deluge and you can feel like you're drowning.

Another description for a "conversation hog" is "conversational narcissism," a term first used by Charles Derber to designate "ways that American conversationalists act to turn the topics of ordinary conversation to themselves without showing sustained interest in others' topics."[2] The following are ways to determine if you are a conversation hog.

SUPPORT VERSUS SHIFT RESPONSES

Derber presented two possible responses conversationalists use to either direct focus on the speaker, or redirect the focus of conversation to self:

1. A "support-response" is supportive of speakers and engages them in a way that connects with them personally.

2. A "shift-response" always redirects the focus of attention in a conversation back to the conversational narcissist.

Derber finds that the "pervasive tendency for individuals to seek predominant attention for themselves" is largely a component of American culture because American culture supports individualism, self-gratification, and encourages self-interest and self-absorption. As a result, far too many business people are far too focused on *their* turn to speak and what they plan to say than on truly connecting with the other person, and largely at their own peril.

Here are examples of the two types of responses in a business setting:

Support-Response

Let's say you're at a networking meeting, standing over by the hors d'oeuvre table, and you overhear the following conversation:

Bob says, "I love a nice cheese tray. It reminds me of the time my wife and I went to Epcot at Disneyworld and enjoyed a delicious cheese plate at a sweet little cafe-style restaurant in the France Pavilion."

Tony smiles and responds, "That's such a great memory. When were you there?"

In this case, Tony picks up on Bob's conversational cue and joins Bob on the path he began by asking a simple follow-up question about Bob's experience. They can easily have a nice conversation going back and forth; or, if Bob is a conversational narcissist, he could keep right on talking about himself, cheese, Epcot, his wife, and so on and never ask Tony a question. But in this moment, Tony's contribution to the conversation is supportive, marking it as a prime example of Support-Response.

Shift-Response

Now, at the same networking event, still lingering by the hors d'oeuvre table—where all the best conversations happen—you overhear the following:

Jennifer says, "I love a nice cheese tray. It reminds me of the time my husband and I went to Epcot at Disneyworld and enjoyed a delicious cheese plate at a sweet little cafe-style restaurant in the France Pavilion."

Melissa squeals excitedly, "Disney is awesome! I remember the first time I went as a kid, Epcot didn't even exist. We go just about every year now and the parks have changed so much! They added a couple other parks now and have that Twilight Zone Tower of Terror thrill ride—it is *awesome!* I love thrill rides. I've been to every park east of the Mississippi and experienced…"

Given the same scenario and opening line by Jennifer, Melissa hooks onto one part of the conversation—Disney—and then quickly turns the subject to herself and her experience at Disney. From that topic, she launches into how much she enjoys thrill rides and after only a few brief seconds this conversational narcissist is happily chattering away—without giving a thought to her victim.

In looking at each of those types of responses, can you see how an elevator speech could be considered a form of conversational narcissism? After all, isn't it simply taking any opening and cramming it with a self-directed, one-sided, one-track soliloquy?

Don't answer that yet. First, here's an example of a shift-response taken from a random training on "How to Prepare an Elevator Speech":

> Marcus says, "This is a great networking event and such a nice location. I always love it when the chamber chooses one of the fabulous restaurants in town for a meeting."
>
> Trevor agrees. "Me too. By the way, I'm Trevor Smith and I help businesses reduce their tax liability. Last year, after reviewing the books of one company, my suggestions reduced their federal and state taxes by 25%. I'm sure I could help your business save money as well. While some of my competitors charge an hourly rate, I use a flat fee so my clients know exactly

what their costs will be. I am currently accepting new clients; may I send you some additional information?

(Note: This response was copied directly, word-for-word, from a Website that purports to teach people how to write excellent elevator speeches. Seriously. No need to make anything up. This is the kind of drivel people are being taught to say out loud to other human beings.)

Trevor's elevator speech, like most elevator speeches, is all about "me, me, me." Although it may seem to Trevor he is focused on "helping" the listener, he has no evidence that Marcus is a business owner, or a decision-maker to help a business who may want to reduce tax liability. Poor Marcus simply tried to make polite conversation, and had Trevor taken the conversational cues—you know, by actually listening—he could have responded with his opinion of the restaurant, how he is a member (or not) of the chamber, or even about the town in general.

Unfortunately, Trevor's statement jumps immediately into how amazing he is with the terribly weak, "by the way" transition. Further, this statement shows the over-confidence of a narcissist by being so "sure" he is the one who could help, when he doesn't know the first thing about Marcus, other than he is at the same networking event. Trevor paints himself the hero of the scenario without even knowing what the scenario is—or who needs "saving"!

ALWAYS BRING IT BACK TO THEM

In another alternative to the supportive-response or shift-response, there is a third style of conversation that I find allows for equal speaking time from both people. Use this simple formula: Talk about them. Talk about you. And *always* bring it back to them.

For example, this type of conversation might go like this:

Bob might say something like, "I love a nice cheese tray. It reminds me of the time my wife and I went to Epcot at Disneyworld and enjoyed a delicious cheese plate at a sweet little cafe-style restaurant in the France Pavilion."

Tony might respond, "That's such a great memory. I bet that cafe was really authentic. Whenever I think of cheese plates, it reminds me of my grandmother who, whatever the occasion, always had a cheese platter, but I don't think any of them were French. Do you remember what cheese you liked best?"

Granted, this conversation starts out about cheese, but could easily move into a direction about work. Let's keep it going and see how that might look:

Bob might say, "Gosh, it's been so long ago I don't even remember the names of those cheeses. The only cheese I see most days is in my brown bag lunch with turkey and Swiss! What kind of cheese did your grandmother serve?"

To which Tony might respond, "Oh nothing as fancy as a French cafe, probably. Just some Wisconsin curds, cheddar, and Swiss mostly. So you carry your lunch every day, huh? Where do you work?"

Bob might answer, "I'm in the big office building over on 22nd Street at the accounting firm there. How about you?"

Tony could respond, "I do graphics for an ad agency not too far from there. Are you one of the accountants?"

Bob could say, "No, actually, I'm a sales rep. Tell me about the ad agency you work for. Have you been there for a while?"

By being supportive on both fronts, the conversation is even and equal and moves back and forth easily. So Bob, instead of launching into his spiel, struck up a conversation completely unrelated to work. As the conversation circled back around to work, Bob decided to start asking questions about Tony's experience at the ad agency.

The accounting firm he does business with usually lands new clients who are mid-size companies that have been in business for three to five years. If Tony has been at the company for 20 years, Bob will know that's not likely a good fit. So now Bob can save the sales pitch in favor of having a pleasant conversation with someone new, who just might have another connection for him.

At the end of the conversation, Bob could choose to tell Tony the kinds of clients he is looking for. For instance, Bob might say, "If you know anyone at a mid-size company that's past the start-up phase who might need some free accounting advice, my company's folks will look over last year's tax returns and see if we can save them any more money."

To which Tony might respond, "It so happens my wife works for a marketing firm that could maybe use that free look-see. Can I give her your card?"

And…boom…they're off to the races!

Obviously, it's easy for me to create a make-believe conversation on a page where I can have my characters say anything I want them to say, steering them in any direction I want them to go. But for illustration purposes, it works out great because you can see how each speaker supported the other in the conversation, yet still found a way to turn talk to business in a friendly way, that in the end benefited both of the people in the conversation.

Not every conversation will end up with a lead or referral. In fact, most won't. But after a pleasant interaction, Tony is much more likely to remember Bob the next day—and beyond. Not because he hogged the conversation from start to finish, but because he made a true connection.

FORM: ANOTHER TYPE OF CONVERSATION

Life, business, and social media relationship coach Gary Loper published an ebook titled *37 Keys to Better Networking Relationships: The Art of Networking,* in which he writes about an easy method to begin and carry on conversations using the "FORM" method.

After a quick Google search, it's clear Gary didn't invent the FORM concept, but he is how I learned about it, so I'd like to give him credit here for teaching me something new so I can now share it with you!

Conversations can easily begin with one of four topics and you can use the acronym FORM to remember what kinds of questions you can ask:

F—Family

O—Occupation

R—Recreation

M—"Message," "Motivation," "Memories," or "Mission" depending on which expert you consult.

It can be helpful to tie your questions in context to the event. For example, if you are attending a daytime event in the summer you could say, "I work out of my home and it's tough getting to a meeting with the kids out of school for summer. I'm lucky to have my parents close by who enjoy babysitting. Do you have kids?"

Remember that these FORM questions are generalized and work in most situations, probably because they apply to most of our lives. You can never go wrong asking about someone's family, their job, what they do in their spare time for recreation, what motivates them, or their favorite memories.

THREE SIMPLE CONVERSATION TIPS

Like I said, it's easy to create the perfect conversation when you can write it down, edit, move things around and create the perfect scenario between quotation marks. But what happens in real life is quite different. When all else fails, remember these three simple conversation tips:

1. Mirror image. If you want a simple gauge for whether or not you're talking too long, try the "mirror image" approach of monitoring how long you speak versus the other person. Keep the conversation equal in the amount of time you and the other person each speak.

2. Talk about similar topics. If the person shares about his dog or kids, you can share about any pet(s) you have, your kids, your grandkids, your nieces or nephews…the conversation topic is about kids and animals so keep it there. This helps keep

the conversation flowing by moving it in the same direction each time, rather than veering off into unrelated topics the listener might not be interested in.

3. Listen. Earlier in the book we talked about how important listening is. When you listen to another person as you're speaking to her, giving her your whole attention, she feels special. This was one of motivational speaker Zig Ziglar's greatest talents: to speak to a person and make her feel like the only person in the room. I had that experience when I met him, even though there was a line of people behind me waiting to speak to him. Zig didn't care a whit. He was talking to me. And yes, I felt truly special, as did everyone in the line after me, who also had their turn at feeling like the only person in the room. This type of listening is a special skill but can be achieved when you apply the same kind of focus to the person you're speaking to.

From these three tips, let's move on to some simple ways you can react if you get stuck in the web of a true conversation hog (aka conversational narcissist):

WHAT TO DO

Unfortunately, with the preponderance of Americans being conversational narcissists due to our cultural upbringing, you're likely to meet many conversation hogs along your road to success. You'll recognize a conversation hog by the fact that all you have to say is one short sentence and then the conversation hog is off and running like Forest Gump crisscrossing the country by foot—never stopping.

So why bother? Why not just walk away and let this conversational narcissist talk *himself* to death? Well, that person may be someone of influence and a person who maybe just talks a lot when he is nervous, as many are in networking or social situations. Being a conversation hog doesn't make anyone a bad person, or even a bad connection, just one you have to work a little harder to get along with—and get a word in edgewise!

If you want to try to make a conversation out of someone else's monologue, you could interrupt briefly to say something like, "That is really interesting. Could you tell me more about X?"

At least this way you get to guide the interaction a bit and can ask a few pointed questions to find out more relevant information about the person. However, after a while, even the best listener has her limits. So, the following are a few tips if you happen to get stuck:

- Common Nonverbal Cues. He can't take a hint if you don't give him one. Look conspicuously at your watch. Glance around the room. Look over the other person's shoulder. He may take the hint and end his story and move on to his next victim.

- Polite Excuse. If it becomes clear that this person is all about himself, is never going to let you engage, and you really want to get away, try interrupting with an excuse to physically remove yourself from the conversation. Pull out your phone and say you've been expecting an important call and that you want to check your messages, and politely excuse yourself. Catch someone's eye across the room and say you need to catch up. Try to be as polite as possible, for as long as possible, but when it's time to pull the rip cord, it's time to pull the rip cord!

- Direct Excuse. Being direct and honest is another good alternative, and you can allow the other person to save face by saying something like, "Oh my goodness! I think we could stand here the whole night chatting like this, but we need to branch out and speak with a few other people while we're here too! Thank you so much for sharing. How about we connect on social media (be specific by offering a particular platform, like LinkedIn or Facebook) so we can stay in touch?" If you have your phone with the mobile apps of your favorite social media, you can send a connection request right then and there while the other person is looking on. It doesn't cost you a dime to be connected on social media, and if you want to keep in touch that way you can. Again, a conversation hog isn't a bad person, and could become an excellent resource for you, and social media is a perfect way to discover more about anyone.

Direct and friendly works every time—this is my personal style—and may just earn you a connection if the person really isn't a conversation hog, just nervous and can respond later with a clearer head.

HOW TO KNOW IF YOU'RE A CONVERSATION HOG

This is difficult because most conversational narcissists will read the previous section very carefully so they know when they can talk again, but will completely ignore this section. However, most of us can fall into the conversation hog category time and again. I'll admit to being guilty of this at times, too.

It can be easy to hog a conversation, even for those of us consciously trying to have a legitimate discussion. When we're passionate about a topic or when we're excited about something or even when we are nervous, it can be difficult to zip it, especially if you have a good listener who seems interested in what you're saying.

But the only people who will listen to another person talk for an hour straight usually get paid as a psychologist or counselor. Beyond that professional setting, even a psychologist doesn't want to listen to a diatribe at a networking meeting or family barbecue.

Pay attention and make sure you are not speaking far too much in a conversation—any conversation, whether with a new connection at a business meeting or across the dining room table at the holidays or a dinner party with friends and family. To ensure that you don't become a conversation hog, here are a few tips to keep you grounded:

- Look for the above cues. Is the other person looking at his watch? Glancing around the room?

Not looking into your eyes and asking questions from curiosity? Then it's time to zip it.

- Be conscious of your own voice. Have you told a complete story from beginning to end and barely taken a breath? Then it's someone else's turn.

- It's okay to apologize. When you realize you've been a conversation hog, take a breath and apologize with as few words as possible and then ask the other person a question and allow her to speak while you actually listen and only ask questions pertinent to her. When I catch myself occasionally being a conversation hog, I do this every time.

Listening is a skill, and one we must acquire if we are to master the fine art of conversation. Hopefully these tools have been helpful in making you aware of conversation hogs, even if it's you!

ENDNOTES

1. Bob Burg's 10 Feel-Good Questions can be found at http://www.burg.com/10-feel-good-questions/; accessed June 8, 2014.

2. Charles Derber, *The Pursuit of Attention: Power and Individualism in Everyday Life* (New York: Oxford University Press, 1979), 5.

CHAPTER 8

ABOUT SOCIAL MEDIA—BECOMING AN INDUSTRY SUPERSTAR

When movie stars like Brad Pitt and Angelina Jolie arrive at an event, there is never a need for introductions because everyone already knows who they are.

Now, we could take a moment and bemoan the fact that our celebrity-focused culture makes superstars out of people who may not even deserve the fame, acclaim, and attention they inevitably get, or we can stop and think about how we "regular people" might have the opportunity to take advantage of that mentality for our own benefit.

SOCIAL MEDIA KILLED THE ELEVATOR SPEECH: SIX STEPS FOR BECOMING AN INDUSTRY SUPERSTAR

Using social media and the various free online tools available to anyone who can get onto the Internet today, you can be just like Brad Pitt and Angelina Jolie within your own world and be so instantly recognizable, there will be no need for introductions.

That's because when you are the talk of your industry, people will simply know who you are and you will never have to introduce yourself again. To make that happen, the following are six steps for becoming an industry superstar using social media.

1. Build and Communicate Your Credibility

Unlike modern-day "reality star" celebrities, most people in business need to show evidence of some talent, skill, education, experience, or background in a particular area in order for others to believe that we are people who should be listened to.

However, it's interesting that it isn't always necessarily the smartest, most qualified, most credible people who are the superstars in any given niche or industry. Instead, it's usually the ones who know how to get the word out to the most people in order to hit critical mass and become a household name within that field, niche, or industry. We call that marketing.

The lesson here is that there will always be someone better, smarter, and even more qualified than you. Put yourself out there anyway. If you have the right qualifications, go for it. And if you don't, you can even succeed in some ares by representing yourself as a "regular person" or "man/woman on the street" who offers "common sense" solutions rather than mere academic theory. There is always a way to spin the amount of experience you have in your favor, you just have to get creative about doing it.

To help build and communicate your credibility, here is some credibility-building information you can share:

- Number of years you've been at what you're doing

- Academic background and educational credentials

- Awards and certifications

- Special talents or skills

- Organizations or affiliations you belong to

- Number of clients served

- Case studies of successful clients

- Testimonials

- Etc.

2. Start Showing Up "Everywhere"

One of the biggest compliments you can get from people in your market is that they see you "everywhere." That means you're making a major impact and an increasing number of "impressions" to increase your visibility.

The goal is to reach a point of saturation in your field. That means you may be appearing on industry-related podcasts, Webinars, and telesummits. You may be getting mentioned in industry-related blogs, ezines, and newsletters. You are talked about on social media, and you have your own content—blog posts, articles, videos—linked by the other celebrities in your industry, niche, or market.

3. Become a Speaker at Industry Events

In addition to those in your market seeing your name in multiple places, they should also *personally* see you in many places in a front-of-the-room role. To achieve this particular goal, you can be a keynote speaker, breakout session speaker, a panelist, an event's emcee, or even an event sponsor (if you're given stage time as a result).

The more you appear on stage, the more you become like a superstar in that particular market. There is just something about seeing someone in a position of authority, live and in person, that screams not just credibility but star status! The people who are at the event will be tweeting and sharing photos of you on stage, quoting your best lines, and saying they had a chance to meet you. For those who can't be there in person, they'll see plenty of photographic and video evidence of you appearing on multiple stages. After the event be sure to use those photos and public testimonials on your own website, social media pages, etc.

4. Stop the Presses

Every industry has its own form of niche media, whether it's nursing or the legal profession or plumbing or nutritional supplements. If you're a newsmaker within your industry, the media will come calling. When they do, make sure to have plenty of written content—articles, blogs, bios, press releases, white papers, and the like—to help them out. If you're sending solid news with interesting stories, you'll soon get noticed by the press in your industry. Once journalists know you're a reliable source, they'll be beating a path to your door for your comment on various events that happen in the industry.

5. Have a Voice of Your Own

The quickest way into oblivion is to be a "me too" person. In other words, the more you're like everybody else, the less you'll stand out as yourself. When you're running against the norm and have something important that is new and different, you'll stand out.

When I decided to write this book, I knew it would be controversial. Kill the elevator speech? Am I joking? *Everybody* should have an elevator speech. At least, that's the popular, "me too" consensus.

By taking a risk and sharing my unique perspective, people may not agree with me, but they will be more likely to remember me—and my ideas—because this isn't just another "how to write an elevator speech" book. Even before the book has been published I've been invited to deliver keynote speeches, and have been interviewed on radio and TV because the topic is unique, helpful, and interesting.

6. Be a Storyteller and Engage Your Market

People. Love. Stories.

They love stories and will be much more likely to remember you if you're a great—or even a good—storyteller. Tell your own personal stories, tell stories of others you've met, and ask people in your market to tell their stories. Oprah Winfrey used this exact technique to launch herself beyond being a local TV journalist and morning show host to becoming one of the most popular and powerful women in media.

How? She understood that telling a compelling story, being willing to open up about her own life, and interviewing others about their stories was engaging. She also always did it in front of a live studio audience and in her early years had audience members ask questions and join in the conversation. Today, blogs and social media allow for that conversation to happen on a much broader level.

USING SOCIAL MEDIA TO KILL THE ELEVATOR SPEECH

I created my Twitter account in late 2007, but didn't really "get it" until at least a year later, in mid-2008. That's when I suddenly realized there was a platform that allowed anyone to talk, quickly and easily, to anyone else who also had a Twitter account.

At that time, there was significantly less clutter and few early adopters. Celebrities, journalists, and business people were trying to make sense of how to best communicate with Twitter. As a result, many celebs were tweeting on their own behalf and happily tweeting back and forth with other Twitter users.

One evening, I was a guest on a colleague's radio show and I tweeted the link for my followers to listen and call in. Within moments, the rapper and entrepreneur MC Hammer, who was one of the earliest celebrity adopters of Twitter and was following me, called into the show and became part of the conversation.

I didn't tweet @ him. I didn't use a hash tag. But because he happened to be online and reading his tweet stream at the time, and because I had interacted with him prior to that moment, he was curious about what I was doing and called in. He stayed on the show chatting for a few minutes before moving on. But that's the power of social media. I didn't have to introduce myself—Twitter gave me 160 characters (that's 20 whole more characters than in a tweet!) to do that on my profile for anyone to read at any time.

Through Twitter I have connected with many fascinating people whom I've never met personally. One of those people was radio show host, author, and coach, Gary Loper, who I "met" only through our tweets. Almost two years and hundreds of tweets and retweets later, I had the pleasure of finally meeting Gary face-to-face at a live event.

Instead of a stilted handshake and how do you do, it was like seeing an old friend, even though we had never met in person.

We instantly recognized each other from our social media avatars and easily picked up the conversation in real life where we left off on Twitter. After that event, we went right back to keeping in touch on Twitter, and later on Facebook as well. Now, imagine having to give an elevator speech in the same scenario.

The point of these stories is that in neither case did I have to walk up to a stranger and do a cold, formal, impersonal introduction. That's because, really, social media is as informal of a medium as it gets. Which isn't to say that it can't be carefully orchestrated and well-thought-out ahead of time. After all, you can "hang out strategically" on social media to meet people in advance of any event you plan to attend. What social media you use does not matter, as long as the people you plan to meet are there and you give them a reason to get, and stay, engaged.

In 2006, not long after I started my business from home, I decided to attend a scrapbooking event. That was before the days of Twitter, and Facebook was still just getting traction with college kids on a few campuses. But there were Yahoo Groups back then, and the scrapbooking conference I was planning to attend, by myself without knowing anyone else, hosted a Yahoo group where attendees—basically 99 percent women getting ready to gather and play with stickers, papers, and glue while learning tips to preserve family memories—could get to know each other in advance of the weekend-long event.

Before "social media" was even a thing, I met a really cool woman on that forum named Chris. We chatted there and both took part in a fun activity where we had "secret scrapbook sisters." Those who participated had to answer a short questionnaire about our likes, interests, location, and hobby. And then, based on the answers to her questions posted on the site, we had to put together a gift basket of items for our "secret scrapbook sister." My secret sister turned out to be Chris, the woman with whom I connected on the site.

The event had about 500 participants in a huge hotel ballroom, and then many other breakout sessions throughout the weekend, where the attendees had to stand in line and wait for the classes to open. While in line we chit-chatted with each other, and interestingly enough, I recognized many of the women from the forum, so they didn't feel like strangers.

I connected really well with one woman in particular—who turned out later to be the very same Chris who I had met online and was my "secret scrapbook sister." We became fast friends in person because we had already met each other online; and although she wasn't aware of it, I had read her questionnaire in depth to be able to shop for her gift basket.

Try getting that kind of connection with an elevator speech!

NEVER INTRODUCE YOURSELF AGAIN: USING SOCIAL MEDIA BEFORE A NETWORKING EVENT

Bottom line? We are social creatures. We crave interaction with other people, and will do almost anything to get it. Take technology: from Skype to Facebook to Tumblr to Instagram, we've found ways to use the technology at our disposal to meet each other no matter where we are in the world.

This is yet another reason we need to kill the elevator speech. Social media has made the need to say everything we can about each other before parting forever obsolete. If you connect with the right people before an event—those who are the connectors themselves—they will introduce you to those they know and soon the conversations will be flowing smoothly.

The following are a few steps to using social media before an event so you never have to introduce yourself again:

1. Show and tell. Before reaching out to anyone, make sure your profiles are up-to-date with a current photograph of your face smiling at the camera, updated links, and that you have a good description of who you are on a professional and personal level. Currently my Twitter profile introduces me as: "Best-selling author, Pro Speaker, Speaker Trainer & Coach, Mom, lover of good food and really happy person. I love roller coasters!" My LinkedIn headline says this: "Speaker, Best-Selling Author of 21 Ways to Make Money Speaking, Public Speaking Consultant." Because LinkedIn tends to be much more business professional, I use only my professional information in my description. I change my description on both Twitter and LinkedIn occasionally to reflect the projects I'm currently working on.

2. Be a joiner. Check the event website to see if they have a Facebook group for the event or a hash tag for use on Twitter and Facebook, too. Tweet and Facebook post from your profile that you'll be attending the event using the hash tag, and ask for others who will be going to connect with you and to become Facebook friends. (Note: LinkedIn used to have an event feature, but as of the end of 2012 they disabled it.)

3. Members only. Groups are a great way to connect with connectors. Check the event website to see if they have their own member's group or forum, and if so begin interacting with others actively there.

4. Facebook it. Go to the event promoter's Facebook page and look for people talking about the event there. Connect and become friends with those who are talking about going to the event, too.

5. Straight to the source. Go to the event promoter's business page and check to see if there is a LinkedIn group. Connect with people there.

6. Topics of discussion. Some topics never go out of style, and are always great ice breakers. For instance: what people will be wearing at the event, when people are arriving, where people are staying, what good restaurants are nearby, and more. I once created an online sensation before attending an event—as an attendee, not a speaker—because I bought a pair of red shoes to wear. Other attendees and folks not even going to the event asked for a photo, and suddenly my new red shoes went viral with the people going to the event. That was in 2009. Now, years later, a couple of those people still occasionally mention my red shoes when they see me or in interactions on social media. (They were fabulously fun shoes!)

PARTING WORDS

As you can see, one way to kill the elevator speech is to be so visible, so credible, so front-loaded, so popular or connected that you truly need no introduction. And we just saw that you don't have to be "Brangelina" to do it! Simply by using the various tools at your disposal, and focusing on your on and offline presence in the right way, you can become a niche expert who truly needs no introduction.

Hence, no elevator speech!

CHAPTER 9

YOUR "MINI" SPEECH
OF INTRODUCTION

Now hold on just a minute! After all the previous chapters, you might be shocked to see that I believe there are, in fact, times when a type of "elevator" speech is both expected and appropriate. But that's just it: it's only a "type" of elevator speech, and just barely! So, what is it? I call it a "mini speech of introduction" because you are, in essence, making a very brief—very focused—speech to an audience.

We define a "speech" as standing in front of a group of people (an audience) focused on you as you talk (a speaker), delivering comments that you may or may not have prepared.

But note the speaker-audience distinction; they are expecting a speech, in this case a speech of introduction, whereas when folks typically use an elevator speech they are just assuming the speaker-audience distinction instead of focusing on having a good, old-fashioned conversation.

There are specific instances where you will be attending a meeting and will be invited or required to share who you are and what you do. Typically, these brief personal introductions are limited to 30 seconds to two minutes. However, make no mistake, those are very specific times and there are some guidelines you should follow to be sure you are still connecting with those who hear your personal speech of introduction.

This chapter examines the few times you will need to introduce yourself to a roomful of people at one time, and how to do so in the most efficient—and memorable—ways.

SCENARIO 1: WEEKLY LEADS MEETING

Having been called the "Father of Modern Networking" by CNN and "Networking Guru" by *Entrepreneur* magazine, Dr. Ivan Misner is the visionary who in 1985 founded the world's largest business networking organization, Business Network International, otherwise known as BNI®. While it's a far cry from being the *only* weekly networking and leads organization, BNI® is the most well-known and largest internationally.

The philosophy of BNI® is predicated on the notion that "Givers Gain®," which is similar to how I have often described public speaking as "serving from the stage." The idea comes from the concept developed by Zig Ziglar, who is famous for saying, "You can have everything in life you want, if you will just help enough other people get what they want."

Having attended several BNI® chapter meetings around the Chicago suburbs, I can tell you the format is similar to that of other leads organizations. During the first part of the meeting, everyone in attendance has the opportunity to introduce themselves to the group. In some groups, each person stands at his or her seat, and in others, the person simply stays seated.

Regardless whether or not you're sitting or standing, this brief personal introduction can be defined as a "speech," and the other attendees fall into the category of "audience" in that moment while you are speaking.

However, this personal introduction "mini-speech" is in stark contrast to the elevator speech's "Make people want to whip out their wallet" approach and is even different from the current iteration to "Be intriguing enough to get them to ask more" approach.

Based on the definition of why the group was formed, the goal of the personal introduction mini-speech at a networking meeting like BNI® is generally to "help others." Networking meetings where business professionals share leads are a place to give by providing support, sharing information, and introducing the others in the group to the rest of your personal network so that everyone in the group benefits and grows.

The purpose of the personal introduction speech is to allow the members of the group an opportunity to *know what you actually do for people.* When you come up with some pithy, yet vague-sounding "elevator speech," you'll leave most of the people in the room feeling confused—or, at worst, suspicious—about what you truly offer.

That serves no one, least of all you.

Remember, if everyone is at a leads meeting with the purpose of giving leads to everyone else, that means you've got to give them a reason to refer you to others so they can give to you. That helps them help you, which is the whole reason why they—and you—are there.

Since my business was in its infancy, I've attended a weekly local independent leads group, founded and led by a Shaklee representative, Deb Villarese. Deb is unlike most other direct sales representatives I've met. She's not a heat-seeking missile looking for her next MLM target. She truly embodies the philosophy of Dr. Ivan Misner, which is also similar to my colleague and personal friend, best-selling author and speaker, Bob Burg, co-author of *The Go-Giver* and *Go-Givers Sell More*.

In the true spirit of BNI®, Deb seeks first to give. And she does so without waiting with her hand outstretched for the return to come back from the person she just helped. She knows that the more people she helps in as many ways possible, the more she will ultimately sell in her business. And that strategy has worked. Over her nearly 30-year career in Shaklee alone, she has netted more than $2 million, gone on countless free trips, driven the cars when Shaklee had a car program, and enjoyed a rich and fruitful career.

The purpose of a leads group is simple and twofold:

- To get leads of prospective customers for your business;

- To give leads of prospective customers to the members of your leads group.

Leads groups are organized so that there is one seat for each type of business represented. For example, in my leads group we have:

- Katherine, the real estate agent;

- Rich, the photographer;

- Thea, the financial planner;

- Joe, the website maintenance guy;

- Stacey, the silk florist and interior decorator;

- Matt, the mortgage guy;

- Mike, the sales trainer;

- Dr. Bryan, the dentist;

- Dr. Erin, the doggie and animal chiropractor (yes, really!);

- Kurt, the home health care services provider;

- Anne Marie, the accountant;

- Stephen, the credit card company rep;

- Jim E., the computer fixer-upper and huge Cubs fan;

- Lyle, the heating and air conditioning guy;

- Kathy, the jewelry direct sales rep;

- Dawn, the insurance sales agent;

- Jim J., the radio ad sales guy;

- Starla, the hand-engraving gifts artist;

- Debra, the estate planning and trust attorney;

- Sue, the custom baker;

- Deb, the group's leader who founded the group about 15 years ago. She is a rep for a direct sales

> company offering vitamin supplements, green
> home cleaning supplies, makeup, and more;

- And me, the marketing, communication, and
  speech consultant.

Over the years I've been a member, we've had other professions represented such as graphic designers, house cleaners, travel agents, bankers, home security experts, moving company reps, artists, massage therapists, and more.

As you can see, there is a diverse group of people who, by the way, I just listed from memory. The reason I could list those people in my group from memory isn't because I have some amazing recall skills. It's because I remember their weekly 30-second introductions to themselves, otherwise known as their mini introductory "elevator" speeches.

You can find leads groups around the world. Some, like the group I'm a member of, are independent and free to join if your category is open, others have a fee to join, an annual fee, or other rules like being a member of another group first. Such groups include one of the largest in the world, BNI®, which, as mentioned previously, stands for Business Network International, founded by Ivan Misner; Le Tip; and leads groups run through local chambers of commerce.

The format to most leads groups is similar, either weekly, biweekly, or monthly:

- Members and guests sit around a U-shaped table.
- Leader welcomes members and guests with an official opening.

- Members and guests deliver their 30-second introductory "elevator" speeches.

- Members pass leads to other members.

- Members from the group are spotlighted as speakers so other members can learn about each other's businesses and who a good referral lead or perfect client might be.

- Some groups invite outside speakers for an educational part of the meeting.

- Group ends with members going around again, each delivering a 30-second promotional for a special or sale or event, their introductory "elevator" speech a final time, or sharing who might be a good lead for them.

One of the benefits of having a polished, rehearsed speech to deliver in a group like this is that by delivering the same speech meeting after meeting, the "regulars" have the opportunity to learn what you do, and have the language they need on hand to refer you to others.

I can hear Joe from my group now, "I'm Joe with Borsche Digital, handling your website maintenance and development. Remember, your website is more than just a pretty face. It may look good, but it has to work for you." (Is that not classic, or what?!)

Of course, one of the downsides of delivering the same old introductory speech meeting after meeting is that, after members have heard it a dozen or more times, you can be seen as unimaginative, lacking in creativity or non-spontaneous.

Keeping your mini-introduction speech fresh can keep people in the group entertained and interested in you—and willing to refer you to others. In my group, some of the things various members have done over the years to keep their 30-second intros fresh include:

- Piggybacking onto others' intros for the day. For instance, Rich, the photographer, might say, "Deb will make you feel good, I'll make you look good…with a great headshot!"

- Tie into current events. In this case, on election or primary day, Mike, the sales guy could say, "I'll show you how to get your prospects to vote with their wallets."

- Talk about upcoming/current holidays. For instance, one jewelry rep used to give us the "countdown to Christmas."

- Tell a joke, rhyme, or a riddle. Stacey, our resident florist, often starts her intro speech with "Roses are red, violets are blue…." By varying the "punch line" to her poem each week, she makes herself both memorable and unique.

There is a unique vibe when meeting with the same people regularly, particularly when the joint goal is always to help each other. One way to help each other, and yourself, is to perfect each other's introductory speeches.

SCENARIO 2:
SEMINAR, TRAINING, OR CONFERENCE GROUP

Regardless of the type of work you do, it's likely that you'll occasionally be in a room where the facilitator or leader will ask those in attendance to share who they are and what they do. It may be a seminar, training session, or "group" setting at an industry conference.

Inevitably, you'll go around the room and be expected to get across in just a few seconds something compelling enough so others in the room want to connect with you. This is where a mini-introductory speech can really pay off and help you share your expertise with those within your industry.

SCENARIO 3:
ONLINE IN FORUMS, USING SOCIAL
MEDIA AND YOUR WEBSITE

While communicating online has many similarities to communicating face-to-face, there are of course some major differences, most notably regarding the mini-introduction speech.

Communicating online is largely asynchronous and, except for video or audio messages and Skype, is largely unspoken. In face-to-face communication settings you have a different context to open a conversation than you do online. In most online settings, you typically only have words and images to build relationships.

This can be a challenge, but also an opportunity. Just like the book version is different from the movie it inspires, both have features and benefits that will appeal to different audiences. The key is tailoring your mini-introduction speech for a specific medium, in this case online.

When you interact on social media, in a forum, or online group, what you could say in a mini-introduction speech would also work in the description of yourself on the group page. For example, your description on LinkedIn should have enough information that a person reading it—who is in your market—would be compelled to connect with you. Likewise, the 160-characters allowed in your Twitter profile is a great way to hone your mini-introduction to its "mini-est"!

SCENARIO 4: IN PRINT

While this use for a mini-introduction speech isn't really a "speech" at all, just as with online communication, you can use aspects of what an elevator speech might entail as more of a "tag line," so to speak. Use this tag line version of your elevator speech in your business card design, print brochure, post cards, etc. If after reading this book you feel inspired to create a new mini-introduction speech, you could actually create an entire marketing campaign around introducing your new phrase!

Consider a three-step direct mail campaign where you announce your new tag line—i.e., one version of your mini-intro speech specifically designed for the print medium—and provide current customers, past customers, and prospects a fresh, new reason to get in touch with you to purchase your products and services.

ANOTHER MINI-INTRO SPEECH OPTION

One of my business mentors, direct mail and marketing strategist Dan Kennedy, talks about an idea he learned from copywriting and marketing genius Joe Sugarman. If you're not familiar with Joe Sugarman, you undoubtedly are familiar with his work and some of the products he created and marketed. Remember those funky BluBlocker sunglasses launched in 1986? You know, that were initially sold using clever infomercials featuring "man on the street" interviews with people trying on BluBlocker sunglasses for the first time?

You might recall one of the ads with a man wearing a sombrero, rapping about how wonderful the sunglasses were. Those sunglasses were invented and marketed by none other than Joe Sugarman. If you've ever dialed an 800-number, you were the beneficiary of one of Joe Sugarman's marketing tools. After all, in the 1960s he came up with this very system to help his direct response advertising clients have a mechanism for prospective customers to call their companies without having to incur an expensive, long-distance telephone bill.

Clearly, Joe Sugarman is one of the pioneers of modern direct response copy and marketing techniques. I've actually met Joe and we shared the stage together at an event in Las Vegas in 2008. He's still working and is still as clever as ever.

Dan Kennedy talks about a strategy he modeled after Joe Sugarman that Dan calls creating a "clever truth" about your product or service. You do this either at business inception or, later, by positioning yourself or your organization as the best, biggest, most "whatever" in the world or country of whatever it is you do. For the strategy to work and be truthful, you must be specific about the category you are in and, as Dan Kennedy says, "Create a category of one for which you are the *only* choice."

Here are several examples of this theory in action:

- Back in the 1960s Joe Sugarman called his company J, S, & A, "America's Largest Single

Source of Space Age Products" because, while his company was likely not technically selling more in quantity than existing giants like Radio Shack or Sears, he was shipping more out of one warehouse location direct to customers—the single source—than any of the others, and therefore was telling a "clever truth." As a result, he uniquely created a genre of one—and his company was it.

- Dan Kennedy modeled the same idea when, in 1983, he declared his new company, Success Trac, "The Largest Integrated Publishing and Training Company on Practice-Building Serving the Chiropractic and Dental Professions." What made this a "clever truth" was that at the time he was the only company serving both markets—chiropractors and dentists—simultaneously.

- Another Dan Kennedy example: From its inception, Dan has called his No BS Marketing Newsletter "The Largest Paid Circulation Newsletter in its Genre." That genre? Teaching direct marketing strategies for non-direct marketing businesses. From his humble beginnings in the first month with only four subscribers, to what is now a worldwide circulation, Dan has always "technically" told the truth. He created a 1-publication genre. So he was the largest—of one.

- After learning this technique, one of my clients, Janet Gomez, a cookbook author living in Geneva,

Switzerland, decided to begin calling herself, "The top vegetarian and Ayurveda nutritionist for women in all of Switzerland." At first she was uncomfortable with the title because there is actually another cookbook author in her market who presents similar information. After we added "for women," however, she felt completely comfortable because her solutions are targeted for busy women, thus a more "clever" truth.

- Another client, Ann Potts, a training consultant in the Chicago area, created this tag line for her company: "Executive Performance Fuel, LLC, Chicagoland's premier training resource for growth-oriented companies with 50-500 employees." Even in a crowded market, she found a way to stand out and specialize in her niche.

After many hours of reflection and in conversations with some of the country's most elite sales trainers, I've learned when you create a tag line using a clever truth, you establish authority in your marketplace, while at the same time being 100 percent truthful about three vital issues:

1. Who you are;

2. Who you help; and

3. What you can do for them.

Keep these in mind as you use your clever truth in your written marketing in place of elevator speech-type language and watch initial interest in your company soar.

YOUR SPOKEN OPTION: SHARE AND TELL

If you truly want to stand out and be empathetic by putting yourself in the other's position, even when you are using a mini-intro, you might consider using part of your 30 seconds to share a useful tip with your audience. Tell people who you are, who you help, and what you do for them and then, if you're a professional organizer, for example, add something like, "Here's a quick tip for you: the quickest and easiest way to keep your paper jungle under control is to stop it from coming in the door. Keep a recycling bin at the entrance to your home. Before bringing in the junk mail, toss it immediately into the recycling bin and your counters and tabletops will be far easier to keep in order!" The fun thing is you can always share the same tip or mix it up depending on the season or what's happening in the news. By sharing your knowledge with the group, you're giving something to your audience. That's when you open the send-receive dynamic and can then receive their knowledge, or access to their connections.

WHEN TO USE YOUR NON-ELEVATOR SPEECH

Now that you understand there are, indeed, a few specific times in your business when you might just need to use a mini-intro, here is a brief rule to help you determine if using your mini-intro speech is appropriate.

Drum roll please. Use your spoken mini-intro speech only when you have been invited to share "30 seconds" or "a brief introduction" about yourself in front of a group where others are going around the room doing the same in an organized fashion.

That's it. Really! Otherwise you're verbally vomiting all over anyone else and it *will* work against you.

Part Three

Perfecting Your Signature Speech

CHAPTER 10

NETWORK WITH A ROOMFUL OF PEOPLE AT ONCE

So far the focus of this book has been about how most people are systematically taught to use their rote elevator speeches at regular networking events. But let's not lose sight of the forest for the trees. For if elevator speeches are mostly worthless, then what's that say about these events? Well, I'll tell you: randomly attending networking meetings is inefficient at best and can leave you victimized by others giving their elevator speeches.

So what's the solution? Well, in this chapter I'll introduce what I call the *Signature Speech*™ and its way better.

SINGLE YOURSELF OUT WITH YOUR SIGNATURE SPEECH

If you've never considered it before, let me be the first to tell you that public speaking as a tool to market your business can provide amazing results. Often, in order to reach the audiences you would like to speak to, you'll have to be willing to speak pro bono—for free. Lots of small business owners worry about wasting their time, however, and not getting adequate return on their investment.

Can they be right? Is it worth standing your ground to get a speaker's fee and risk losing the speaking gig? Or is speaking for free an entryway into a new, larger, potentially more profitable market?

In an effort to answer those questions, let me start by responding to another question I get from a lot of folks: "I always charge for my talks. My rate is very reasonable, $50 per hour, plus prep and travel time. It usually works out to about $100 per hour of actual speaking time. My question is: do you suggest that I *not* charge for my talks? This seems counter-intuitive to me, so that's why I'm asking. Since I'm a one-person business, and this is also my 'day job,' I want to earn money wherever it's appropriate. So that is really my question: is it appropriate to charge for my time?"

This was my actual response:

"I love that you charge for your talks and get it. That's another realm, however, than the Signature Speech. The purpose of the Signature Speech is to gain access to your ideal target market as a featured expert in order to give them a taste of what you offer and get more business.

"You should have just one speech you deliver pro bono— that is, for free. If you have been successfully charging for your talks, by all means continue to do so. But the Signature Speech is designed to be a marketing tool to help you reach groups you may not be able to reach without a free speech.

"Many groups have no budget for a speaker and rely on business experts in the community to come in for free. I, like you, am a one-person business, and I'm also a paid professional speaker. Speaking in itself can be a lucrative career, but I designed the Signature Speech particularly for nonspeaking professionals to expand their subscriber lists in a hurry—and possibly bring in more cash on the spot.

"Although I never charge to present my own Signature Speech, I often leave events where I delivered my speech for free with money in my hand due to immediate sales at the event. Of course I make residual sales days, weeks, and months after the event due to regular and consistent follow-up.

"I suggest you create one presentation you deliver for free. Then consider the time you spend at the events as marketing time—like going to a networking meeting, but *you* get all the attention. You wouldn't expect someone to pay you for attending a marketing event like a networking meeting. In fact most people expect to pay to attend such an event.

"However, as the featured speaker you get in for free and get to run the room. Instead of running around shaking everyone's hand individually, you get to say hello to everyone at once during your speech. It's a whole new world! And so worth your time in immediate and later results. When you meet others in this context, you'll soon see the power of marketing your business with pro bono public speaking."

You can totally circumvent the whole elevator speech thing *and* have every single person in a room full of people you'd want to network with by doing one thing.

POINTS FOR GIVING YOUR SIGNATURE SPEECH

The Signature Speech is something that I created and have the trademark on—so there isn't anyone else in the world who can teach the complete system to you other than me or one of my certified trainers.

So, what is it? The Signature Speech is a persuasive presentation you deliver to an audience of your ideal target market used as a marketing tool to build credibility, generate leads, and quickly add cash to your business.

Think about it: at your typical networking event, you can generally only meet a dozen or so new people, one on one, and that's if you really hustle and work the crowd. But with a public Signature Speech, now instead of having to walk around the room one at a time talking to as many people as you can, you get to spend 30 to 40 minutes or more talking to every person in the room. What's more, there will never be a "What do you do" question because you're up there on stage teaching about it.

Obviously, you want to have your own Signature Speech ready because, unlike the elevator speech, public speaking has been proven to work in the real world—and around the world—by thousands of my students for building a highly targeted, highly responsive list of raving fans who actually feel they know you, simply because they heard the answer to "What do you do" for a full half hour or more!

You could never get away with a 30-minute "speech" in a one-on-one situation—and you wouldn't want to. Folks tend to zone out after only a few minutes, and 30 full minutes would feel like pure torture to them—and you. But delivering your own Signature Speech to the whole room is like you've been *invited* to use a megaphone and people are grateful to you when you do it right. Of course, do it wrong and you might as well have a megaphone in the corner of the room or verbally vomit an elevator speech on people because they don't work either.

First, a quick definition from my landmark ebook, *Cash in on Speaking,* found at: http://www.CashInOnSpeaking.com:

Your Signature Speech is a persuasive presentation you prepare to market your business to a live audience filled with your ideal target market.

While the speech *is* persuasive in nature, you will give plenty of information while you deliver it, as you'll see in the next few chapters. The culmination of your speech asks your audience to do something, and so that is what makes this speech persuasive by definition.

Don't worry. You won't have to coerce anyone to do anything. In fact, if you provide enough information, your audience will want to sign up for what you offer because they know it's going to help them.

CHAPTER 11

NINE SIMPLE STEPS TO CREATING YOUR SIGNATURE SPEECH

Public speaking is one of the most powerful ways to market your small or home-based business. Combining instant name recognition, credibility, and celebrity status—what's not to like? Savvy entrepreneurs everywhere realize the power of a well-crafted presentation to get them more prospects, more clients, and more referrals.

So why aren't more people giving Signature Speeches more often? Intimidation can have something to do with it. No one ever went broke giving seminars to folks with fear of public speaking, and even those of us who don't cringe in front of an audience can be daunted by the challenge of crafting a Signature Speech worth remembering.

To that end, here are nine steps to get started with using a speech to market your business and be successful with this powerful marketing technique.

STEP 1:
DETERMINE YOUR TOPIC

Consider what those in your target market, audience, or niche most want to know more about. Don't just pay "lip service" to their needs, really put yourself in their shoes and consider what they would want to hear given your expertise, skill set, and case studies.

Craft a Signature Speech to remember, not one that's immediately forgotten because you chose a boring, overused, or overly simplistic topic or approach.

STEP 2:
DO YOUR HOMEWORK

Since this is you we're talking about—your time and experience and expertise—you may only have to go as far as your own bookshelf for details to add to your Signature Speech. You'll want to pack your presentation full of useful information to share with your future audiences, so do your homework and give them facts, case studies, personal stories, statistics, and figures that help them learn something useful and valuable.

STEP 3:
ORGANIZE YOUR SPEECH

One thing about speaking is that the audience only knows what you tell them so give them something worth hearing and easy-to-follow. In other words, create a speech that is well-organized, logical, and flows seamlessly.

Start with a compelling attention-getter such as a question, an anecdote, a fact or figure, and lead your audience through your speech in a logical progression. One method is to share some problems people you work with typically face and offer a variety of possible solutions—in addition to working with you, of course.

STEP 4:
OFFER SOMETHING FOR FREE

You want to be able to make contact with your audience in the future. So offer a free report, white paper, ebook, elearning course, resource list, video series, checklist, or follow-up action guide that you will send via email in order to collect the contact details of your audience members.

To avoid becoming a nuisance, make sure they know you will stay in touch with them and how to unsubscribe if they no longer want or need your information.

STEP 5:
GET SCHEDULED

As you are preparing your speech, connect with event and meeting planners to get on their schedules as soon as possible. Have a simple document ready that tells them your topic and the top three things the audience will learn, receive, or experience as a result of your talk, as well as your bio. If the group has a website, blog, or social media presence, request that your speech information is posted there as well so you still have exposure to even those in the organization who are not able to attend your presentation. (Most event planners do market you in this way, but I've found it's good to ask them, because sometimes they may not and will be happy to do so simply because you asked!)

STEP 6:
PRACTICE (A LOT)

Now that the event is getting closer, it's time to bring your speech to life. To begin, practice your speech—out loud (not in your head!)—from beginning to end. Time yourself so you know exactly how long your speech will take to complete, and make sure it's well within the event's time-limit guidelines. Don't forget time for questions and answers, especially if the planner has requested it.

Meeting planners will tell you how long your allotted time is. Do not go over or under that time by more than one to two minutes as there is usually a good reason for the time limit, and you don't want to "burn your bridges" with a valuable organization and/or audience out of sheer ego or poor planning.

STEP 7:
GIVE THE SPEECH

Go to the event polished and prepared, feeling comfortable and confident you have something of value to share—because you do! Pay attention to the details and learn to get comfortable with the crowd. It might be a big deal to you, but think of all the speakers you've seen in your time and remember how little you cared if they flubbed a line or had shaky hands.

In the end, knowing your stuff, practicing, rehearsing, and being really passionate about helping others will shine through; that's what they'll remember the most, so remember to give it to them!

STEP 8:
FOLLOW UP

After the event, follow through promptly and professionally. If you promised materials, either to participants or the organization holding the event—or both—send them right away. When you do, ask for referrals and offer a product or service in your follow-up communication.

STEP 9:
KEEP IN TOUCH

Effective, regular, and consistent communication is what will keep you top of mind and provide you with the most opportunities to generate sales down the line. Make sure your contact contains more useful information such as resources, discounts, articles, insider secrets, or other details people like to receive.

PARTING WORDS

If you're a visual learner like so many of my clients, you can watch a YouTube video I created based on this portion of the chapter. Visit: http://FeliciaSlattery.com/9steps.

CHAPTER 12

THE TOP SEVEN MISTAKES ENTREPRENEURS MAKE

As a communication consultant, speaker, and coach, one of the problems I see is too many small business owners who think they know what they're doing when it comes to using public speaking as a marketing tool. Unfortunately, time and again, entrepreneurs, solo professionals, sales professionals, and small business owners make the same mistakes.

Are you ruining your chances of marketing success by wasting precious speaking opportunities making the same mistakes over and over? If you're not getting the results you want from your public speaking, you may be making some of the following mistakes.

THE FIRST MISTAKE: NOT HAVING A CLEAR OFFER

Never forget the audience's needs, or that you're there to help. The details of your speech should do that, and so should the offer you present to your audience. If you're not clear on what people will receive, or even that you have anything specific to offer, they will be confused and therefore not sign up. Remember, a

confused mind always says "no." So be sure to provide clarity so
that they can say "yes" instead.

THE SECOND MISTAKE:
NOT PRESENTING YOUR OFFER WHEN
YOUR AUDIENCE NEEDS TO HEAR IT

Delivering a good speech is all about timing. If you aren't
timing the presentation of your offer properly, you'll lose a major-
ity of your audience simply because it's either too soon, too late,
or buried somewhere in the middle. With a well-organized, well-
rehearsed Signature Speech (see previous chapter), you will know
the right placement of your offer, which will be embraced by the
audience, each and every time.

THE THIRD MISTAKE:
NOT PROVIDING ENOUGH DETAIL ABOUT
THE BENEFITS OF YOUR OFFER

Don't dance around the offer. You must be explicit. Why would
people want what you offer? Tell them what's in it for them. How
will their lives, businesses, careers, finances, or relationships be
positively impacted by taking advantage of what you have to offer?
Be specific. It's okay. They're already there for what you have to
offer, now you just have to give it to them …without beating around
the bush.

THE FOURTH MISTAKE:
NOT PROVIDING ENOUGH HELPFUL INFORMATION
DURING YOUR PRESENTATION

Before you offer anything, you have to prove you know something. Some speakers mistakenly believe they can give away "too

much" information during a speech. Ask yourself this: is it possible for an audience to learn everything there is to learn about your subject in one 30-minute talk? Not likely. So relax; they won't learn it all and then ignore you because you have nothing left to offer. Be generous with the information you provide, and you will see the reward in more clients, more prospects, and more cash flow.

THE FIFTH MISTAKE: DELIVERY PROBLEMS

When you struggle with various aspects of delivery, you end up with the worst possible outcome—not being fully connected with your audience. When your audience does not feel a connection with you, they likely won't feel a reason to participate in your offer. So practice, practice, practice, even if it means speaking in front of non-targeted groups a few times just to get the hang of what you're saying, why, and especially how. Once that connection is there and you—and the audience—are really feeling it, the extra effort will surely be worth it.

THE SIXTH MISTAKE: NOT SPEAKING TO AUDIENCES IN YOUR IDEAL TARGET MARKET

If you're not speaking to the right group of people in the first place, they aren't likely to want what you have to offer. For example, if you're a parenting coach with great tips on handling toddlers and grade-schoolers, speaking to empty-nesters or residents of a senior center won't get you the results you want. Meanwhile, a group of local soccer moms would eat it right up!

THE SEVENTH MISTAKE: SOUNDING LIKE A SALES PITCH!

Your Signature Speech should not feel like a 30-60 minute sales pitch, or even an extended—God forbid!—elevator speech. If you don't provide solid, usable information during your talk, why would someone want what you offer? People are turned off by someone they perceive as too "salesy," particularly if they're expecting something informative, educational, and inspirational.

PARTING WORDS

If you are making any of these mistakes, stop now. You could be losing more clients and credibility than you gain by speaking publicly in the first place. When you avoid these top seven mistakes, you'll soon experience all the benefits of marketing your business with public speaking.

CHAPTER 13

NO, YOU CAN'T GIVE AWAY "TOO MUCH"

When you put together your Signature Speech, you'll deliver valuable information to groups of people who fit your ideal client profile—for free. But the question often comes up: "How can I deliver a powerful Signature Speech and provide good information that my audience can use without *giving away too much?*"

I get it. You don't want to give away the shop and then make your service or product unnecessary. In fact, many experts will caution you not to say "too much." I've commonly read advice that states, "Tell people the 'what' and the 'why,' but not the 'how.'"

I respectfully, and adamantly, disagree.

And here's why: your Signature Speech is typically delivered during a 60-90-minute meeting of a group who has invited you to join them as their "special guest." As the featured speaker, you may have the floor for anywhere between 25-50 minutes. Unless it's possible to tell an audience *everything* you know in less than an hour's time, you can relax. Realistically speaking, you didn't get to be an expert by only knowing 25-50 minutes' worth of material, did you? Of course not, or you wouldn't be an expert in business for yourself!

That being the case, you can rest assured. There's no need to worry about "saying too much" or "giving away the shop."

FIVE REASONS WHY YOU WON'T BE GIVING AWAY THE FARM DURING YOUR NEXT PRESENTATION

1. *If it took you this long, how long is it going to take them?*

It's likely impossible for you to tell any audience all there is to know even about one aspect of your small business during a speech in less than an hour's time. Think about how long it took you to learn what you know. Weeks? Months? Probably more like years. Thirty minutes is barely scratching the surface.

2. *Most people suffer from information overload on a regular basis.*

To even attempt to give an audience everything during your Signature Speech, delivered in such a short time, would only confuse and overwhelm them. So don't even try. Instead, pick your favorite "highlights" or focus on a single topic or two and deliver them with pizzazz.

3. *In your Signature Speech, you will give a few vital facts—once.*

Most people need to hear or see information more than once and in multiple formats before they will fully understand and be able to effectively implement what they have learned. For added value, you can offer to follow up your speech with an ebook, ecourse, special report, or product for sale to help enhance the message you presented.

4. *Give a good overview of what people can do right away to get started with what you suggest.*

In my own Signature Speech on how to increase business by communicating your credibility, I give my audiences specific steps they can immediately use to boost their credibility and therefore make more money.

5. *Focus on the basics.*

You can easily lay out an entire system in a few minutes without giving too many details. Consider this more like an "outline" than the full novel, and you'll see what I mean. Those who want to know more and get your expert advice on implementing your suggestions, steps, tools, and techniques will be those who become customers. Everyone else will be thankful for your information and may become referral sources.

As you can see, there really is nothing to worry about when it comes to giving away too much information when you deliver a speech to market your business. By giving away a few juicy tidbits, people will wonder what wonderful information will come after your Signature Speech.

CHAPTER 14

GET YOURSELF BOOKED

When I tell people that I train entrepreneurs and small and home-based business owners all about putting together what I call a Signature Speech to market their business, one of the most frequently asked questions goes like this, "Where is the best place I can go, locally, to deliver my speech?"

Here it is, one of the absolute best places to begin.

Are you ready for it?

Drum roll, please—your public library.

THE BEST PLACE IN YOUR COMMUNITY TO DELIVER YOUR SIGNATURE SPEECH

Yep. The library. So simple, yet often overlooked. I bet you drive by it dozen or more times a month, never stopping to think that, inside, is a gold mine waiting to be explored. The public library is a beacon of knowledge for your community. And there you can be the ray of light about your topic, giving them the knowledge they need.

Here are the five reasons why I think your public library is *the* best place to start marketing your business through speaking:

1. *Free publicity.*

Libraries do their own publicity. Some libraries have a newsletter, a regular featured column in the town's newsletter, or a news and events section on their website and more. Further, local newspapers are more likely to post events at the public library, because it's typically a free resource their readers would love to discover, so that's yet another way you get publicity for your business, your name, and your topic. All for free.

2. *Libraries present community outreach programs on all kinds of topics.*

Just like you, your local library wants new "customers." Public libraries like to host speakers so they can draw people into the library who might not otherwise have come. Because public libraries are funded by taxpayer dollars, the library exists to serve the public with a wide variety of special interest topics. When patrons come to see you speak, the library has the opportunity to display and showcase the materials found in the library related to your topic and can therefore better serve the community.

3. *Boost your credibility.*

When you are the speaker at an event, you establish yourself as an expert in your field. By virtue of the fact the public library is hosting you to deliver your Signature Speech, you are in essence being endorsed by the library. As a result, people will listen more closely and see you as the expert you are.

4. Become the go-to person in your community.

Even those who do not attend your speech at the library will see the promotional materials the library marketing person creates for your speech, particularly if you arrange the event with a built-in long lead time. When your name is "out there" in regard to being an expert in your field, oftentimes this can be even a month in advance, people will take note—even if they can't necessarily attend. You could easily get prospects and customers simply from the promotional efforts alone.

5. People want to know more, so it's easy to build your list for follow up.

Those who attend events specifically for the purpose of learning the material being presented will typically become the best warm prospects for your business. If you provide valuable information to them during your presentation, they will be interested to learn even more. This is your opportunity to collect follow-up details from your audience members and begin a relationship with them.

When you speak at your local public library, you create a win-win-win situation: for you, for the library, and for the patrons who get to benefit from your information.

AFTER THE APPLAUSE: FOUR EASY STEPS TO GETTING BUSINESS AND MAKING MONEY FROM YOUR SIGNATURE SPEECH EVENTS

Sorry to sound like a late-night infomercial…but wait, there's still more! In order to maximize your results, your follow-up work begins right after your speech is over—even before you leave the event. Here is what you should do after the applause:

1. *Immediately following your speech.*

Take the time to shake hands with everyone waiting in line to speak with you. Sounds easy, right? The challenge is some folks want to tell you their life story while there's a crowd waiting—and looking at their watches. Politely, and sincerely, say, "I would love to know more about this. Can I call you later today (or in the morning) to hear the rest of the story? There are a few people who I know have to get going, and I want to say hi to them, too. Let me make sure I have your card. Is this the best number to reach you?" And then follow up within 24-48 hours. The life story could lead to a lifetime client!

2. *Get business cards from everyone you meet and speak with personally.*

It might sound old-fashioned, but maybe that's because it's so effective. Send those people who gave you a business card a special follow-up greeting after your speech so they know you remember them. Since they've opened the door by handing you a card featuring their phone number and possibly even their address, you can call them directly or send a hand-written note. Direct mail is making a comeback as a follow-up strategy. Don't you love getting "real" mail that's not a bill?

3. *Call those who have detailed questions.*

These are the people who are telling you, "I want to know more!" If they have detailed questions, they may want to engage with you privately. If you are a consultant, you can easily have a new client from this alone.

4. *Pay it forward.*

Finally, in your follow-up communication, tell people about your next free event and give them a taste of something you offer.

Think of it as a bonus free gift for engaging with you that not everyone at the event will receive. It can be a free report, an article you've written, an ecourse, a link to a video, even a resource list. It's been my experience that people get excited about resource lists in this context so they don't have to do the searching themselves to find out more about your area of expertise. A simple book list of recommended reading is often appreciated.

Of course to get to this point, your speech needs to be delivered with passion and purpose. Your speech should also follow the correct Signature Speech format and follow the tips from previous chapters to maximize your results. When you do, coupled with these four follow-up steps, you'll see how easily and quickly your business can benefit from marketing with public speaking.

"PICTURE THEM NAKED" AND OTHER STUPID TRICKS TO GET OVER PUBLIC SPEAKING JITTERS

Nervous first-time public speakers have long been told a number of "creative" ways to help them get past the fear of public speaking. As a speech coach, communication consultant, and a professional speaker myself, I can tell you these creative bits of advice designed to help you get over being scared are not only stupid and ill-informed, but will likely hurt you and make you feel worse.

In no particular order, the following are the three most common—and silliest—ways these old wives' tales tell to get past feeling nervous. When you hear these, run from the person giving the advice and DO NOT LISTEN! (Sorry to yell, but as you can tell I feel quite strongly about all this.)

1. *"Picture them naked."*

This seemingly pornographic advice refers to imagining your audience in some position that lowers their perceived power. Other variations on this theme include, "Picture them in their underwear" and "Picture them on the toilet." To all of these (and especially the last one about the loo), I say, "Ewwww." And how distracting! Not only do you have to remember your speech but now you have to visualize people in unflattering positions? No thank you.

What's better: Visualize yourself delivering your speech calmly and confidently. And as for what to do with your audience? Look at them as people interested in hearing what you have to say and strive to make a connection with them, one audience member at a time. Oftentimes reducing a larger audience into individual members is the best way to "picture" them as people first, a mob second (or better not at all as a mob!).

2. *"Instead of making eye contact look at their foreheads/chins."*

Or "Look at the back of the room." (Really?) People *do* notice if you're not looking them in the eye. Unless you are in a very large auditorium on a stage far removed from the audience, people will be able to tell if you are avoiding eye contact. And then they will not trust you, and you will lose rapport quickly. It's beyond unlikely that delivering your Signature Speech for free as you market your business will ever be to a room larger than a nice-sized hotel ballroom, and most commonly it's to smaller groups of 25-50 people.

What's better: Find people sitting in the audience who seem genuinely interested in your presentation and speak to each one individually during your speech. The more eye contact you make with these individuals, the more it will draw others into the presentation as well.

3. *"Start off with a joke."*

Only start your presentation with a joke if you are a priest, rabbi, or minister delivering your weekend talk/reflection/mediation/sermon/homily...or a comedian. (That kind of sounds like a bad joke itself.) Or begin with a joke if the joke is completely relevant to your speech. But if you feel nervous speaking to a group, it's not a good idea to lead with humor. Starting with some random joke will only lower your credibility during the first 10 seconds when audiences are making their first impression of you. Then what if they don't laugh? What if you offend or alienate half the audience? Then you'll be feeling more uncomfortable with your audience right off the bat. If they don't laugh, well now you're even more nervous because the first thing you planned bombed.

What's better: Start with a compelling story, rhetorical question, or interesting facts. Yes, of course you can use humor during your presentation; you just want to be sure it makes sense in the context of your speech. And if you're not the witty comedian type, relax. Just be the fabulous you that you are and be willing to share your knowledge freely.

If these four alternatives don't work, then you may be asking, "What *is* the best way to get past my nerves?" Here it is: Practice and prepare. Visualize your speech going exactly as you want it to go. And strive to make a connection with your audience by paying attention to them.

Remember, delivering a speech is not about you—it's about your audience and giving them what they want during your public speaking presentations. All the tricks, tactics, and "secret" strategies can't replace a well-prepared, well-intended presentation by someone who actually cares enough to show up bringing their A-game!

You Don't Know Me, But I Know You: The Power of "Silent Subscribers"

Of course, the goal of networking and speaking to market your business is to become a recognizable authority within your niche, industry, or local geographic area, depending on what you do. We want to know and develop relationships with all kinds of people, for example:

- Potential customers or clients;

- Reliable vendors with products and services to help your business;

- Joint venture partners;

- Affiliates and those willing to help promote your business to others;

- Colleagues who offer products similar to what you do (it's always nice to "talk shop" with someone who gets what you do from the inside!);

- Community, market, and industry leaders;

- Fans, friends, and people who support you and your message.

By continuing to expand your message, you'll soon develop many of these kinds of relationships. Before you know it, you'll be like one of the popular kids in school, being invited to all the cool "parties" (networking events and seminars), and people will know your name and all about you.

Maybe they follow you on social media or visit your website or read your blog; or perhaps they have heard you on radio shows or podcasts or webinars; or maybe they read your information in one of your affiliates' email messages about you—or maybe they're what I call a "silent subscriber" in your community.

A silent subscriber is a person who has subscribed to your newsletter or email list, but with whom you have had no personal interaction. The longer you are in your business or your profession, the longer this list of silent subscribers will be. We like silent subscribers, because they represent untapped potential and supporters.

Case in point: one day you'll be at a networking meeting or other event and one of these friendly silent subscribers or social media fans will recognize you, approach you, and start talking to you like you're old friends. They are already quite comfortable with you and, as a result, a lot of that awkward initial feeling and conversation isn't there at all because they feel as know they know you. (No elevator speech needed!)

However, there's one problem with this: You don't know them. They have you at a disadvantage because suddenly you're in a position to have to ask who they are and what they do to learn about them. Often people in this situation will introduce themselves and tell you how they know you (something along the lines of, "I've been reading your newsletter since I heard you on that podcast last year with Karen Jones…"), but then they stop there with the introduction.

It's not likely they will deliver you their elevator speech because they feel as though they know you already; when we know someone, vomiting a pre-determined word-for-word diatribe on a respected friend is not our first instinct. Even so, if you happen to mistakenly ask that horrid trigger question, "What do you do?" you could be at risk for the very thing we're trying to avoid.

Remember to ask the personal questions addressed earlier about how they got started or the favorite part of what they do.

On the flip side, what if you happen to recognize someone you follow? Here are the simple steps you can follow to introduce yourself:

- Introduce yourself: "Hi, Shannon! I'm Felicia Slattery."

- Tell the person how you know him or her: "I've been reading your blog for the past two years!"

- Prove it politely: "I loved last week's post about being newsworthy. I had never thought about holding a contest, but I want to give it a go."

- Engage: "What would you say is an example of a great contest you've run or seen for speakers and authors like me?"

This simple process can help save you a lot of time, energy, and embarrassment by formulaically mining for information that can help you be on even footing, even if you've never met before.

CHAPTER 15

WAYS TO CONNECT MEANINGFULLY

Since beginning back to work after open-lung surgery to remove the cancerous tumor in my lung and air passage, I decided to add something new to my business. I call it "Connection Fridays." Curious? Come on, you're a smart cookie, I bet you can guess what that means: that's the one day a week I take to *consciously connect with those in my community.*

During this unique venture I've connected with past mentors, past and current clients, joint venture partners, potential affiliate partners, and friends old and new. Some had strategic agendas they wanted to discuss and some just wanted to do some old-fashioned catching up. In my business, catching up can often lead to excellent things because both sides of the conversation sound like this, "How can I help you?" It's always such fun!

Another form of connection is about doing something nice and possibly unexpected for someone else. So on Fridays I also make sure to write and record testimonials.

TESTIMONIALS: THE POWER OF GIVING

I love giving testimonials for service providers and product creators who have provided an excellent service or have a product that not only delivers on what it promises, but may even do more. The recipients are always so happy and grateful.

One of my own mentors, marketing consultant Steve Sipress, saw my post about my Connection Fridays and the testimonials I give and instantly suggested that I speak to his group, Chicagoland's Sharpest Entrepreneurs, a few weeks later. Not only that, he also wanted me to create a product that covers all the details anyone would need to know in order to both get and give excellent testimonials.

Although creating that kind of product wasn't necessarily in my production schedule, I added it quickly because there are so many people who have asked me how I am able to quickly and easily record videos and write useful testimonials, often on a moment's notice.

Testimonials work as an excellent way to connect with someone else because they benefit the receiver and you as the giver.

In talking about using testimonials for your business, most of us initially think about getting testimonials from our happy and satisfied clients and customers. However, ancient teachings from a variety of sources abound about the principles of giving and receiving being intricately intertwined. No training that focuses on one but not the other could ever be complete.

For proof, let's look at some of the history behind this universal principle of giving and receiving being tied together.

- Chinese philosophy teaches that the "yin and yang" are complementary forces, interacting to form a whole greater than either separate part; in effect, a dynamic system. Therefore, you cannot have giving without receiving because they are, together, part of the same dynamic system.

- In biblical teachings, this universal truth is written about in both the Old and New Testaments. In Proverbs 3:27, it says, *"Do not withhold good from those to whom it is due, when it is in your power to do it."*

- And Luke 6:38 tells us, *"Give, and it will be given to you. A good measure, pressed down, shaken together and running over, will be poured into your lap. For with the measure you use, it will be measured to you."*

- And finally, Second Corinthians 9:6-8 explains, *"Now this I say, he who sows sparingly will also reap sparingly, and he who sows bountifully will also reap bountifully. Each one must do just as he has purposed in his heart, not grudgingly or under compulsion, for God loves a cheerful giver. And God is able to make all grace abound to you, so that always having all sufficiency in everything, you may have an abundance for every good deed."*

Bringing the concept into modern teachings, Bob Burg and John David Mann, authors of *The Go-Giver* and *Go-Givers Sell More* (both of which should be required reading for any business owner) discuss the fact that before you can sell anything, you must first give value. Their model is based on the simple premise that "Shifting your focus from getting to giving is not only a nice way to live life and conduct business, but a very profitable way as well."

Clearly, wherever and whenever you look, giving and receiving are inextricably tied together.

FIVE BENEFITS OF GIVING TESTIMONIALS FOR CONNECTING—AND MORE

When you take the universal truth related to giving and receiving and apply it to how you run your business today, you end up with some powerful principles that will benefit you as well as those to whom you give. Therefore, we'll first focus on giving excellent testimonials so you can be open to and ready to *receive* excellent testimonials.

The First Benefit: You Open Up the Sending and Receiving Dynamic

As you've just read, this giving-receiving dynamic has been described for centuries and without one—giving—you cannot successfully have the other—receiving. Give excellent testimonials first and freely; then be open to receive. The principle may not be *exactly* like a cosmic bank account where you put something good in and get something good in return, but regardless of the teachings you follow, apparently it's pretty darn close!

The Second Benefit: You End Up with a Grateful Product or Service Provider

"So what?" you ask. "So what if someone is grateful for my testimonial? What do I get out of *that?*" Well, here's so what: people remember when others do good for them. The next time you go into your local print shop where you posted a positive review, you could find that you get a 10 percent discount; or when the nice lady at the coffee shop you stop by every morning knows you gave her a positive review on Yelp.com, she'll make your medium size into a large. Getting more of what we like is a good thing, particularly when you get to help others in the bargain!

The Third Benefit: People See You as Articulate

When others see your testimonial posted as a video on a website or they read a well-written text-based review that you've given, unsolicited, you raise your own status in the marketplace as an articulate person with an opinion and something important to say. It shows you are attentive to other people's value, which says offering value is something important to you as well.

Interpersonal communication teaches that we are attracted to those we see as possessing good communication skills and abilities. An excellent, well-delivered testimonial breaks the ice and can open up the lines of communication.

The Fourth Benefit: You Get More Exposure and Name Recognition

The more testimonials you begin to freely give to others, you'll start to get this type of reaction: "I see you everywhere!" And it's true: your name, photo, or video will be featured on other business websites, blog posts, brochures, ads, email promotions, and more. If we're talking about getting "sticky," it doesn't get stickier than this. And, using the "know-like-trust" model, people knowing you is the first step to them doing business with you.

The Fifth Benefit: You Get Hired and Make Money

As more people begin to see you and you get that recognition, particularly if you are writing testimonials in your industry or geographic area, the effect of you looking articulate and clearly understanding the importance of providing value and a positive customer experience can lead to those in your market seeking you out, especially when you follow the formula you'll learn next. The formula makes it easy for your potential clients to find you.

Okay, so now we've seen how to *give* testimonials—and why. Now it's time to find out how to *ask* for testimonials:

ASKING FOR TESTIMONIALS: A USER'S GUIDE

One of the places I love to ask for testimonials is on social media. People are used to sharing their ideas, thoughts, and opinions using social media, so it's an easy, logical, and strategic decision to ask for a testimonial for your products and services on your favorite and most visited social media site(s).

In fact, LinkedIn even offers a built-in tool to provide testimonials for those with whom you're connected. It's called "recommendations"—not to be confused with those crazy "endorsements." The difference is that recommendations are actually written testimonials structured by LinkedIn. Sometimes I find the categories and the forced choice options the site makes you select aren't always the exact perfect fit. However, the tool itself is familiar to professionals of all kinds, so it's an easy type of testimonial to both give and get. Plus, another bonus is that rather than receiving the testimonial privately via email, it's already "out there" in public, on the Internet for all to see. You didn't make it up or fake it; it's in the exact words for all to see.

ASKING FOR TESTIMONIALS AS A GROUP LEADER OR MEETING PLANNER

As the planner or facilitator of a meeting, networking, or otherwise, you have a lot of control over each aspect of your meeting or event. You decide the tone of the meeting, the rules of engagement of the meeting, the format of the meeting, the placement of chairs around the meeting space, the speaker (or none) of a meeting, and so much more to determine the style of communication at any meeting.

You set the tone for what will happen at the meeting and what you choose to do—or not do—will allow the participants to connect with people meaningfully or make them fumble about.

With great power, of course, comes great responsibility. If you've ever run any kind of meeting or event before, then you know the people in the room will have you to praise—or blame—for the structure and productivity of the meeting. Even if the purpose of your meeting is something as simple as a regular networking meeting or as complex as a multiday conference or seminar, those who attend want a return on their investment, whether that investment was in time alone or in money, too.

As a speaker, I have had the pleasure of speaking at dozens, if not hundreds, of networking meetings over the years I've been in business. I've also been an attendee at many events as well.

Most of the time, meeting planners of such events tend to be more concerned with the food, event program, and registration table rather than looking at all those elements as pieces in a larger "audience event experience" puzzle.

While those pieces are certainly important, there is one element that, regardless of *all* those other things, people will continue to come back to experience again and again—the connections they make at those meetings.

For a firsthand account of how to do event planning right, here are two examples of events done well:

1. Naperville Area Chamber of Commerce Women in Business: Monthly Local Meeting

The first is a monthly networking meeting run by the Naperville Area Chamber of Commerce, in Naperville, Illinois. I was invited to speak there. In fact, I planned my cancer surgery around speaking for that group. I spoke to them one day and was in surgery the next. Once a month, the Women in Business Group meets for breakfast, and they have a very specific format.

There are a handful of women on the committee who run this organization. On the day of the event, each of them wears red as well as a special name tag so they are easily recognizable, even across the hotel ballroom room to each other. Every one of the 100-150 women in attendance wears a name tag as well. However, any women new to the event (or the chamber) are given a yellow name tag to wear, so they are also easily identifiable.

The committee members see it as part of their job to find the guests wearing the yellow name tags and welcome them to the group, walk around the room with them a little, and introduce them to a few of the other regular members and committee members.

This strategy works well because when someone else is introducing you, you don't have to introduce yourself. As a result, much of the initial discomfort and awkwardness that tend to keep folks away from these meetings in the first place simply… fall away.

These introductions are easy because the committee members all know each other and know most of the regular members too, so when they introduce the new guest, they tell the guest,

"This is Pam Albrecht. Pam runs a marketing consulting company here in town."

And now, suddenly, the guest knows just enough about Pam to strike up a conversation. Here's what we know about Pam in that simple, one-sentence introduction:

- Pam runs her own business. She is an entrepreneur. There's a place to start a conversation, whether you are an entrepreneur and business owner or not. You could say something like, "Oh great! I run my own business, too. I love being able to set my own hours, don't you?" Or, "I've always wondered what it would be like to have my own business. How long have you been doing it and what's your favorite part?"

- Pam is in marketing. What connection do you have to marketing? There's sure to be something, even if it's just about your favorite social media site, so…start a conversation about that.

- Pam's business is in town. The town, in this case, happens to be Naperville, Illinois. Yet another point of connection. People at that meeting would be from Naperville or one of the other close suburbs and can talk about how it's such a great place to run a business. Or you could ask if her business has an office location and where. Or you could ask if she lives in Naperville too, and talk about how it's been named as one of the best towns to live in.

- Pam is wearing a red blouse. This means she is on the committee. You can talk to her about that experience; how long she's been on the committee, what her role is, what she enjoys most about the committee and the chamber, etc.

All that, from less than a minute introduction! Beyond the personal introductions, the next thing that impressed me about this group is they facilitate conversation even after members and guests are seated. They do this a few ways:

- Holding the meeting at a time when food can be served and people can be seated. It's a breakfast meeting. And yes, 7:30 A.M. is early, but for most of us, once we're up and moving, it's a great time of the day to be networking. So there are a few quick talking points—about the time of day, breakfast, and breakfast foods. Also, I've rarely sat down at a table where there are multiple glasses, coffee mugs, side plates, and the like where some of the conversation doesn't fall to table etiquette and which plate and cup belongs to whom.

- Appointing a table leader. Each red-clothing wearing committee member sits at a separate table and acts as the table's leader or hostess. She welcomes the attendees, and steers conversation, taking the onus off the rest of us!

- Planning for guided conversation. This is one of the best things I've ever seen at a networking meeting. Of course, in advance, the leaders know who the speaker is and what the topic of the presentation will be. So they prepare a simple "focus question" each table leader asks everyone at the table. And then they guide the conversation as each person gets a chance to answer the question. Everyone also gets to introduce themselves and pass around their business cards to everyone else at the table, but this part of the conversation is guided and is all about the question of the day. It engages the audience with the topic in advance of the speaker and gives them something to talk about while at the table and even after the speaker's presentation at the close of the meeting when there is always more time for networking.

Even in advance of their meeting, the Women in Business group does something smart: they record a brief two to three minute video message by that upcoming meeting's speaker and send it to all the members of the organization.

That allows the members a chance to see the speaker so that, at the meeting, it almost feels as though they have already met the speaker. For those who see the video, there's yet another instant way to start a conversation with someone you know for sure will be in the room.

As you can clearly see, a large part of the success and size of this group is due to the fact that they plan it so well, and allow for excellent networking to take place, easily and effortlessly for all the attendees, whether guests, regular members, or committee members.

2. Novice to Advanced Marketing System Event (NAMS): Semi-Annual National Conference

The second example of an event where many attendees and speakers return on a regular basis is held in Atlanta, formerly twice a year; once in August and once in February. Beginning in January 2015, it will be moved from Atlanta to a ship on a marketing cruise for the winter meeting, staying in Atlanta in August. It is an Internet marketing conference I have had the privilege of keynoting twice, and in 2013 became an instructor in the breakout sessions as well.

The creator and chief architect of NAMS is David Perdew, a former newspaper journalist, editor, and publisher, who has been an online marketer and entrepreneur since 2005 with more than 2,000 websites and a dozen membership sites.

David is one smart meeting planner. As of this writing, he is planning NAMS 14—that is to say, the 14th time he is running this same conference over several years. In Internet marketing events, making it to 14 live events, hiring all the speakers, filling the room to capacity with 200-300 people each time, and running as many sessions with as many speakers as he does is unheard of. Sure, there have been large Internet marketing events that happen regularly, but never to the size and scale—with many of the same people returning time and time again.

The people keep coming back to NAMS for several reasons:

Effortless Organization

NAMS is organized by skill level, much like a college course of study is organized. The 100-level track features breakout sessions for those who are brand-new to Internet marketing and they spend their time in the workshop doing everything from the very beginning of building an online business: they are taught where and how to buy a domain name otherwise known as a URL—and they *do it;* how to get and set up a hosting account—and they *do it;* how to install Wordpress on their hosting account—and they *do it,* etc.

The 200-level track is for people who already have all that in place and are ready for some strategy to start making money with their new online business. The 300-level track is for those who have been making some money online and are looking for more intermediate marketing skills to break through to business sustainability.

Finally, the 400-level track is for the advanced marketers who have successful businesses and are ready for other skills, such as public speaking (that's what I taught at NAMS 10).

This works for networking because when people go through an experience of working together toward a shared goal, it creates a bond that is unlike other conference and networking experiences.

Instant Bonding

The people at each level get to know each other from doing the work side by side and there is instantly a reason to talk, share, communicate, relate, and remember one another. There is no need for an elevator speech when everyone is starting at square one:

- "What domain name did you buy?"

- "What do you think you want to do with it?"

- "Did you get that last step?"

- "Hey, Mike, I want to talk to you about doing a webinar together for your people."

The advanced people tend to know each other because they have been around the industry a while and the newer folks get to mix and mingle with everyone at every level because it's not a mega-sized event.

NAMS Feels Like a Family

Time after time I've heard people continually refer to the NAMS event as getting together with their "work family." The event starts with pre-event activities on a Thursday, with many people arriving from all places in the country on Wednesday. Workshops continue through the weekend and end on Sunday afternoon.

Almost everyone is in the same hotel with each other, day after day, eating in the same restaurant, riding the same elevators (no speech needed!), and hanging out in the same lobby and bar. You spend that much time with the same people and it really *does* start to feel like family. You don't merely "network" with family. You talk to them and hang out, which is a completely different feeling and brings a whole new familial, positive energy to the event as a whole.

Continually Evolving

NAMS continues to evolve based on actual members' feedback. The NAMS event was originally called the Niche Affiliate Marketing System until David heard the feedback enough times that the event is so much more than "niches" and "affiliate marketing." So he made it broader and changed the name to reflect the true scope of the event.

Another example of responding to feedback was the time when a good number of attendees and instructors at the event were excitedly talking about karaoke and went out to a karaoke place one evening, which I may or may not have had a part in planning, ahem. At the very next NAMS, David picked up a sponsor and they hosted a free karaoke night right at the hotel for all the attendees and instructors to mingle, enjoy themselves, and sing like they do in the shower!

Forget the elevator speech—hand me the microphone! There's no need for that weirdness or marketing pitch when you're enjoying yourself in a casual environment. Yes work comes up—all the time, in fact—and it's easy and just flows because that's the vibe in the room.

Room to Grow

NAMS allows for the opportunity to step up. Like a corporate organization promotes from within, this conference of independent entrepreneurs provides workshops for attendees to learn and implement proven strategies. When they are successful, they move up through the levels to assume more responsibility and enliven their growing skill sets.

After folks have reached the 400-level, they might even be invited to become an instructor at the live event or for the online community through one of the weekly webinars. This provides a strong incentive to keep coming back; and when people do, they continue to see many of the same faces and they get to know each other.

Great After-Party!

NAMS offers connection opportunities well beyond the live events. Granted, people who work online are more likely than others to interact online anyway, but David has made it easy for the interaction to take place. He has setup Facebook groups specifically for his faculty members and another for attendees (faculty members are encouraged to check in there, too).

He uses social media to keep members of both groups up-to-date on the latest news related to the live event and community so that instead of only connecting twice per year, "the family" can keep in touch easily all the time.

For all these reasons, and because the event is well-organized and well-planned, instructors keep coming back, as do attendees, time and time again. Powerful networking happens. And it's because of how the event is planned.

How to Plan Your Events

Doing business successfully is all about the relationships we can cultivate. Bottom line: the more positive, authentic relationships we have with those in our own industry, market, geographic area and so on, the more successful our businesses will be.

Building relationships trumps everything else—period. So if the food is another cold scrambled eggs breakfast or rubber chicken lunch, the speaker is boring, and the location is a little out of the way, attendees will be forgiving and even come back for more at the next meeting—if, and only if, they saw a return on their time and financial investment through the relationships they were able to create and enhance.

Of course, every meeting planner wants their events to go smoothly. They invest time and energy into choosing the right location, the most delicious food items to serve that fit the budget, and find excellent speakers to fill a program. The right speaker can be a draw to a meeting, but if the topic isn't of interest to a particular individual, she may not be motivated to attend.

As a result, many meeting planners struggle to boost meeting attendance at regular networking events. On the other hand, some people will still attend a meeting regardless of any of the extra "stuff" because they want to connect to the other folks who will be there too.

Ask yourself, what makes the difference between a successful meeting you've attended that you will add to your calendar every time it's available and one that is just so-so or felt like a waste of time?

I'll bet it's not because the event had peel and eat shrimp or an open bar or even a life-changing speaker (although I can hold out hope about the awesome speaker!). Rather, it was because of the other people in the room you met, enjoyed meeting, and look forward to seeing again—or meeting others like those people at the next meeting or event.

When an event planner can facilitate that kind of feeling, by not only allowing the natural interaction we all have a tendency to crave as human beings, but by nurturing it and creating opportunities to meet others in a meaningful and fun way—*that's* when your attendees will see your event as successful.

When they focus beyond the puzzle pieces, the best meeting and event planners seek to create a complete connection experience among their attendees. But you have to be creative to make it work.

Fortunately, I have been to a few meetings where the planners did give some thought to exactly how attendees can connect with others by facilitating planned interaction, as I shared in the previous examples. However, the biggest failures with this I've seen came by lack of imagination and understanding that it's not just meeting people in a blab and grab, slam as many business cards into as many hands as possible way.

While activities such as contests to see who can collect the most business cards from others in the room certainly encourage *interaction* to an extent, whenever I've seen this done, only a handful of bright-eyed, enthusiastic competitive types have actually played along while everyone there for serious business reasons rolled their eyes.

This type of activity does not encourage *connection*. In fact, running around the room and grabbing as many business cards as possible and tossing yours out to any hand that comes within three feet of yours provides the same results as the hideous elevator speech—and often accompanies said horrific elevator speech, making the practice completely unbearable for anyone it is thrust upon.

Instead, let's give your attendees a reason to rave about your meeting or event, and want to come to any subsequent meetings as a result. The ideas I'm about to present will work at the following types of meetings or events:

- Monthly networking breakfast or lunch meeting

- Annual conference or seminar

- Chamber of commerce targeted interest group meetings

- Industry trade show

- Organization in-house meetings

- Holiday parties (professional and for families and friends!)

- Association meetings

- Club meetings

And probably many more, but these seemed appropriate for our needs—for now. As you grow and thrive by killing the elevator speech and replacing it with more truly interactive and connective events, you're sure to add events of your own.

IDEAS FOR CREATING INTERACTION AND CONNECTION

Now, on to the activities:

Activity 1: Human Scavenger Hunt and Autograph Game

Activity Description: Hand out a form for every attendee with instructions for the game. In this game, attendees search for others in the room who fit the criteria of each item on the scavenger hunt list and have the person who fits the description sign their name on the accompanying line. The one question not allowed is any form of "Are you any of these?"

Why this activity works for connection: Attendees will have to ask questions about other members to determine more about the person and if they fulfill any of the scavenger hunt items.

Those who complete the game with all lines signed, get their business card entered for a drawing to win a valuable prize.

The following are some example questions for the scavenger hunt. Find someone who:

- Has been in business (or with the organization) for the longest/shortest time

- Has been in business/with the organization for the same amount of time as you

- Was recently featured in a newspaper, magazine, or newsletter

- Has green eyes

- Has the same color eyes as you

- Hates chocolate/pizza/other popular food

- Is left-handed

- Has written a book

- Has visited all 50 US states

- Has the oldest website

- Has a birthday in the same month as yours

- Went to the same high school/college/other as makes sense for the group

- Took the same train/plane/airline etc. to arrive at the event as you

- Speaks two languages other than English

- Loves to read the same genre books as you

- Has the same favorite food/restaurant as you

Or be creative and come up with questions that work or make sense for your event. Use these as starters and add more as you go—and grow.

Activity 2: *Two Truths and a Lie*

Activity Description: Ask each person in the group or at a table to think of two true business-related facts about themselves, and one lie. Each person in the group takes a turn telling the group their three items.

The group then has to agree on which part they think is a lie. Once the group announces their decision, the speaker tells the group the correct answer. The group then can talk about any of the interesting things they just learned about the new person and can connect later with everyone else and already have a point of conversation to begin.

Activity 3: *Business Card Bingo*

Activity Description: First, as attendees enter the room, they place their business cards into a bowl. Each attendee is then given a "bingo card," and the recipient writes her name in the center square.

Next, attendees circulate with everyone throughout the room. To complete the card, attendees must meet 24 other people, collect their business cards, find one thing they have in common (other than obviously being at the same event), and have them write their names in the open squares.

Later, someone calls off the names on the business cards that everyone dropped in the "bingo bowl" when they arrived. Regular bingo rules apply thereafter. The winner is the first person with five names in a row, either across, down or diagonally. This person receives one of the many door prizes that are often given at these events. Of course, everybody really wins, because everyone makes new contacts through the fun process.

Your purpose is simple: help people in the room avoid asking, "What do you do?" and instead get to know each other better so the conversation and connections flow more easily and freely.

Of course, you can plan any of the other activities that were discussed in the example groups: a table focus question, assigned leaders introducing guests to others, a karaoke party, purposely grouping people of similar interests or skill levels that apply to your meeting, and so on.

Parting Words

What's great about truly connecting is that it erases the need for the elevator pitch in the first place. True connections, those that lead to lasting relationships, aren't built on 30-second pitches or rehearsed speeches. They come from interaction, and as you've just read, the more the merrier!

ACKNOWLEDGMENTS

Gratitude. It's one of those emotions that feels so heartfelt and sincere, and in many ways words have difficulty expressing the depth of that feeling as fully as it is felt. That's true for me, anyway. Yet because in this moment on this page I only have words, I would like to thank a small army of people for helping me see this book to its completion.

First, thank You and glory to God for giving me the breath in my body and the gift of the miracle of life and a renewed healthy body, again. When I prayed for a sign that I should keep doing this work, You wrote me a literal job description. Good plan, as always.

To the team and publishers at Sound Wisdom, thank you. Especially Nathan Martin, who kindly and enthusiastically accepted my idea for this book and was so accommodating; David Wildasin, who met with me for hours on the phone discussing our plans and ideas; John Martin for your careful in-house editing of my manuscript; and Angela Shears for your vigilant attention to even the tiniest of details and correcting my sad attempt at endnotes. To all of you: your patience is rivaled only by Job in the Bible.

To Michael Port, thank you for giving me that "Hallelujah chorus" moment of inception for this book that day at Dr. Mollie Marti's event. The lesson for all of us speakers is we never know exactly how we'll impact the lives of the people in our audiences, but to realize we can cause ripples for years to come. You do that every single time you take the stage in all the best ways. You certainly did with me. I am so grateful and truly honored you presented the Foreword to this book, especially because you created the title.

To my cover artist, business partner, and dear friend, Tony Laidig, designer extraordinaire, thank you for your vision for the cover, for including me in the process, for your constant brilliance, and the gift of your friendship. Thank you also for creating my book trailer video and shooting video footage in the elevator that day with Lou Bortone, who also rocks. We have some fun times!

To Rusty Fisher, my editor and "finisher," this book would be barely readable without you! I handed you 40,000-ish words filled with half-written stories, less-than-fully-developed ideas, and a mess of research quotations and citations, and you turned it into something I can be proud of. I am so very grateful for you, the work you did, and your kind and gentle patience with me and my oft-scattered brain!

To those who took the time to read and endorse my book prior to it being printed, thank you. I know you are all incredibly busy people and you amaze me with what you are able to do in service to the world.

To my assistants: Ruth Martin, thank you for your research, organization, and ever-necessary gentle nudges to get you what you need to keep me on track; and Anita Johnson, thank you for getting my KillTheElevatorSpeech.com site and all my sites doing what they're supposed to do online. Without you both, you know how lost I would be.

To my graphics team at Go Wallaby, and your leader, Nathan Woodbury, thank you for your quick and clear design of my very own model of transactional communication, which appears in this book, along with your design and continued support for FeliciaSlattery.com. Your whole team is a treat to work with.

To my colleagues, accountability partners, writing coaches, cheerleaders, and friends: Shannon Cherry, Kristen Eckstein, Tina File, Bob "The Teacher" Jenkins, and Kamin Bell Samuel, thank you for continuing to push me gently yet firmly to my goals and providing the space for me to succeed. I'm sure many times we talked I sounded like a broken record, "I'm working on it, I'm working on it." Well, now, thanks to you and the others here, I can say, "I got it done!"

To my marketing mastermind buddies and our fearless leader, Steve Sipress, at Chicagoland's Sharpest Entrepreneurs, thank you for your ideas, your suggestions, and your never-wavering support.

To my Prayer Warriors, too many to mention all, and so many I've never even met in person, but especially Lou Bortone, Lisa Braithwaite, Dr. Ellen Britt, Austin Erwin, Alicia Forest, Roz Fruchtman, Kathleen Gage, Sharon Gibson, Laura Gonzales, Connie Ragen Green, Daniel Hall, Marie and Michael Herman, Jeff Herring, Kathryn Hoffman, Cynthia Lay, Lynne Lee, Robert

Lee, Dr. Mollie Marti, Kelly McCausey, Chad and Carly Parkhill, Blair Parkhill, Janis Pettit, Victoria Prestia, Luanna Rodham, Nicole San Jose, Therese Sparby, Julie Ann Turner, and Jon Wendt. Between you all, I knew each time I posted in my Journey to Health Facebook page I'd have your cheers and energy. Because of your prayers and the prayers of people around the world, I was blessed with a miracle that not only allowed me to survive cancer and to thrive, but to get back on track to finishing this book.

Finally, to my family: my husband, Brent Parkhill, and our girls, Grace and Miranda, for letting Mommy do the work I need to do, cleaning the interminably messy kitchen, being quiet when I needed you to, and playing together nicely (most of the time!). To my parents, Joan and Keith Slattery, and sister, "Aunt Dana" Slattery, for getting the kids out of the house for trips to the museum, the park, the pool, the movies, and the endless sleepovers, so I could work a few hours so much of the time. Without your love and support I couldn't get to do what I love to do and fulfill my mission and purpose. Thank you also for giving me a soft place to fall. You are my personal heroes. I love you all.

ABOUT FELICIA J. SLATTERY

FELICIA J. SLATTERY, M.A., M.Ad.Ed., is on a mission to motivate, inspire and train smart business owners and entrepreneurs to create meaningful connections through effective communication and public speaking. An internationally acclaimed, award-winning speaker, best-selling author, and the creator of the trademarked Signature Speech™ system, Felicia presents to audiences large and small on topics related to communication, speaking, and being a successful entrepreneur in spite of everything life can throw at you.

As a cancer survivor, Felicia's enthusiastic passion for communication is contagious because she knows that one important message delivered with power can transform a life. She works with experts and entrepreneurs, as well as CEOs and celebrities to help them more effectively communicate their messages on and off stages while building and maintaining strong relationships locally, nationally, and globally, both in person and virtually using the Internet.

You can find out more about Felicia at FeliciaSlattery.com.